SINGLES ALIVE!

SINGLES ALIVE!

by Jim Towns

PELICAN PUBLISHING COMPANY
GRETNA 1984

Library of Congress Cataloging in Publication Data

Towns, James E.
  Singles alive!

  Bibliography: p. 137
  1. Single people. 2. Self-acceptance. 3. Single
people—Religious life. I. Title
HQ800.T68 1984   305'.90652   83-23777
ISBN 0-88289-421-8

The Singles Alive! Declaration on pages 129-131 is from *The Challenge of Being Single* by Marie Edwards and Eleanor Hoover. Copyright © by Marie Edwards and Eleanor Hoover. Reprinted by permission of J. P. Tarcher, Inc., and Houghton Mifflin Company.

The Johari Window of Awareness concept on pages 19-24 is from *Group Processes: An Introduction to Group Dynamics* by Joseph Luft, by permission of Mayfield Publishing Company. Copyright © 1963, 1970 by Joseph Luft.

Verses marked TLB are taken from *The Living Bible,* copyright © 1971 by Tyndale House Publishers, Wheaton, IL. Used by permission.

Manufactured in the United States of America

Published by Pelican Publishing Company, Inc.
1101 Monroe Street, Gretna, Louisiana 70053

This book is presented
in gratitude to God for life and joy;
in appreciation to my family and friends for their love;
and in honor of Mr. and Mrs. Verney Towns

CONTENTS

Chapter Three   Revelation

Chapter Four   Resolution

Chapter Five   Renewal

Chapter Six   Reconstruction

Chapter Seven   Release

Chapter Eight   Rejoice

ACKNOWLEDGMENTS

No one ever writes a book alone, regardless of what the title page might assert. It is not possible in syllable and in sentence for me to express adequately my appreciation for the influence and concern of the many people who have encouraged me in this work.

I am indebted to the "prayer warriors" who consistently prayed for me while I was writing; to Cliff Allbritton, for counsel in writing the manuscript; to Kent Pate, for sharing many of his spiritual insights from the Scripture; and to the individuals with whom I have come in contact whose ideas have slipped unconsciously into my lifestyle—perhaps to have surfaced here as my own. Special appreciation is expressed to David Calhoun, Wendy Long, and Pelican Publishing Company for their assistance in presenting these ideas to you.

INTRODUCTION

Many books about single adults have flooded the market, and there will be many more. Yet I believe that this book is a special contribution to our understanding of the ever-present problems of self-awareness, self-acceptance, and the value and dignity of the single adult. This book is for anyone who has been, is, or ever will be single—and that means *everyone!* I hope that *Singles Alive!* will provide you with some new insights.

A great deal of excitement was generated in one of my university speech classes last semester by a student asked to make an impromptu speech on the topic "As a man thinks, so is he." The impromptu assignment demanded that the student walk to the front of the class, repeat the assigned topic, and speak in a meaningful way. The student slowly walked to the front of the class, turned around, and gave a profound speech. He boldly proclaimed, "As a man thinks, so is he. I think I am through with this speech, so I am!" At that point the speaker returned to his desk. He really became what he thought.

Scripture boldly proclaims of man, "For as he thinketh in his heart, so is he" (Proverbs 23:7a KJV). Many single adults are directly or indirectly experiencing the truth of that verse. If you consider yourself inferior, your actions will reveal your thoughts; you will actually present yourself as inferior. If you think you are okay, then you will behave in a manner that is considered okay.

Singleness is often described in terms of dual possibilities: voluntary or involuntary, temporary or permanent, comfortable or uncomfortable. Regardless of your marital status, you will become whatever you perceive yourself to be. Many singles seem to be suffering mere existence rather than enjoying living.

Isaiah 61 proclaims that there is good news for the suffering and afflicted, comfort for the brokenhearted, and liberty for the captive. To all who are mourning, the Lord God will give beauty for ashes, joy instead of mourning, and praise instead of heaviness.

I have never met a single adult who has not experienced trials of "ashes," "mourning," and "heaviness" in life. Yet these problem periods do not have to be the end of meaningful life; they can provide new beginnings. Each person is God's creation seeking to become all he is meant to be.

My knowledge and understanding concerning single adults have emerged from five major sources:

Personal experience. As a single adult, I have experienced single living in a predominantly couple-oriented society.

Experiences others have shared with me. As I speak at seminars, conferences, and conventions—as well as in my counseling work—I glean many insights from the experiences of others.

Observations and reflective thinking. I have learned to ask, "Why and how do things happen?" Many insights and answers are revealed through spiritual analysis.

Knowledge and understanding of the Scripture. The Scripture gives the basic fundamentals concerning life and living with oneself and others. The Bible gives specific answers to specific problems.

Illumination of the Holy Spirit. The Holy Spirit illuminates and empowers the believer to know things beyond the realm of human understanding.

SINGLES ALIVE!

Chapter One
REALITY

Singleness and a Sense of Value and Dignity

fher

A single person must develop a sense of wholeness in his singleness and an understanding of his own value and dignity. This is often extremely difficult to accomplish, since our society traditionally uses marriage as an indicator of one's worth. However, our culture is gradually beginning to accept singleness as a credible lifestyle.

With marriage the norm of our society, it is not always easy to develop a positive sense of singleness. A single adult often fails to develop self-identity because of a poor conception of who he is. One of the saddest quotations in literature is Thoreau's statement "The mass of men lead lives of quiet desperation." Many singles are living in quiet desperation, without thinking of developing positive concepts and attitudes.

There are a number of steps in key areas that singles should take to build healthy attitudes.

Develop a meaningful personal sense of singleness. A properly adjusted single is not anyone's "better half"; he or she is an individual well-balanced whole. Do not misunderstand: I am not against marriage! I simply mean that marriage must not be an "escape" from singleness. Singleness provides time to develop personhood.

Develop an ability to be alone without being lonely. Everywhere that I speak, I find people of all ages and backgrounds who are trying to find help adjusting to aloneness and loneliness.

Loneliness, a longing for companionship or a feeling of isolation, happens when a person lacks the inner resources to be alone. Some people dread being alone, because loneliness always follows. Others enjoy aloneness as a "quality time," when they can enjoy their own company.

Develop life goals and fulfilling vocations. Immediate goals, for things to accomplish within one year, and long-range goals, usually for five to ten years in the future, should be carefully mapped out for both work and personal pursuits. If a person is not fulfilled in his job, he will be frustrated in other areas of life. Since the normal single spends many hours at work, it is imperative that he find his niche in the working world.

Develop a financial plan to achieve security. A sound financial plan should direct income, spending, and saving. It is a sound financial idea to stay out of debt. There is wisdom in never using a credit card without paying the entire balance at the end of the month.

Remember: the way a person uses his material resources gives evidence of his commitment to Christ. Within the "nuts and bolts" of an individual's practical budget are the values of what he really believes. As God has taught me about finances, he is teaching me about giving. God is also teaching me that I cannot outgive him!

Develop proper attitudes toward dating, commitment, and possible marriage or remarriage. I do not know if I will remain single all my life, but I will accept marriage if it comes or singleness if it stays. Both married people and singles appear to suffer from a grass-is-greener-on-the-other-side-of-the-fence syndrome. Whether married or single, many people view others in the opposite status as if they "had it made." The grass might be greener on the other side of the fence, but you can be sure of these things: the water bill is higher, and tall grass is hard to mow. I have discovered that for every single who thinks that marriage would solve all his problems there is a married person who thinks that being single again would solve all *his* problems.

The Inner World of Singles

Every human being has basic needs that must be met in a realistic way so that he can know fulfillment. First and most basic are physiological and safety needs. Physical needs for food, water, clothing, shelter, and comfortable temperature must be satisfied before the individual can consider any other needs. Safety needs such as security, self-preservation, and freedom from danger hold a paramount place until they have been met.

Relational and social needs are also important. This category includes the need for love and acceptance as well as for social activities. These needs involve family, loved ones, friends, and groups with which a person identifies himself. In the modern world, increasing mobility and the breakdown of the traditional family has made it more difficult to meet relational needs. Singles consequently need to build relationships with other singles and participate in a variety of social activities.

When love and acceptance needs are met, esteem needs, which are expressed in the quest for education, material goods, power or influence, and recognition become important. In other words, esteem needs show themselves in the desire to "be somebody." Some educational needs can be met by singles' programs that present seminars, conferences, lectures, and activities that deal directly with the needs of singles.

Finally, spiritual needs are crucial. Singles need spiritual direction and instruction in an atmosphere that is warm, positive, and nonjudgmental, and they require encouragement to fulfill their spiritual potential. The world's priority is to meet physical, relational, and esteem needs and then give time to spiritual things, but this is reverse order. A person should be spiritually concerned first and trust the Lord for all the other things. Jesus proclaims, "Seek ye first the kingdom of God, and his righteousness; and all these things shall be added unto you" (Matthew 6:33, KJV). As spiritual needs are satisfied, a person starts becoming more of what he is meant to be.

Dealing with Self Realistically

The terms "personal identity," "self-concept," or "self-image" describe who a person consciously or unconsciously thinks he fundamentally is. The most important step in dealing with self is to strive for an accurate self-image. While there have been many books and articles written on this subject, I hope that a review of these basic issues will be helpful for you.

The origin of self-concept comes from what "I tell myself about myself" and what "you tell me about me." It begins with what my family and friends—essentially authority figures and childhood peers—tell me about who I am. My family and friends literally transferred to my mind their evaluations of me as a person, and I began to see myself through their perspectives, feelings, and actions. Day by day I gradually gleaned attitudes from myself and others and from these attitudes and experiences with others I began to compose my self-concept. Some of the experiences might have been forgotten long ago; nevertheless, they influence my thinking and feeling about myself.

It is easy to understand how the atmosphere and attitudes of home, family, church, school, and friends contribute more to self-image than any other influences. The general atmosphere of these attitudes is internalized to form one's self-image.

One of the major problem issues arising from self-image is the development of healthy—and scriptural—self-esteem. The person who approves of himself and feels good about himself most of the time has high self-esteem; the person who usually disapproves of and feels bad about himself has low self-esteem. It is important to understand the difference between self-esteem and pride. Esteem pertains to the conviction that God created man in his own image and instilled in man a sense of personal value and dignity. Pride pertains to man's pleasure in himself for what he thinks he has accomplished with his life. In other words, self-worth is a person's confidence in who God has made him; pride is pleasure a person takes in himself for what he thinks he alone has achieved. Thus, a growing sense of value and dignity draws one closer to God, and the sin of pride leads one away from God to self-worship.

Many people flounder near the extremes of self-love and self-hate, but both attitudes are unhealthy because they reflect absorption with self. Adults should have outgrown narcissism, yet many have not. Christian singles, however, must learn to manage excessive self-love. Tendencies toward self-interest are normal and automatic in human experiences, but the Christian needs to be alert to the dangers and pathological extremes of self-love in himself as well as in others.

Self-Awareness

The first step for a person to become all he is meant to be in relating to the Lord God and others is to be aware of self. The Johari Window of Awareness graphically represents the relationships an individual has with himself and others.[1] The window is simply a square with four quadrant areas, each of which represents a particular type of relation to self and others.

The open area (area 1) represents the behavior and motivation that is known both to self and to others. It shows the extent to which an individual can freely give and take, work, and enjoy experiences with others. The larger this area, the greater is the person's contact with reality and the more apparent his abilities and needs to himself and to his associates. This area can be described as the quadrant of openness, honesty, and frankness, but it does not represent naiveté. In other words, my open area is what I know about myself and want other people to know about me as well.

Johari Window of Awareness

	Known to Self	Not Known to Self
Known to Others	**1** Open	**2** Blind
Not Known to Others	**3** Hidden	**4** Unknown

Behavior and motivation that is not known to self but is readily apparent to others is blind (area 2). The simplest illustration of something in this quadrant is a mannerism in speech or gesture of which a person is unaware that is quite obvious to others. This can take the form of a facial twitch or a frequently used expression such as "you know." A person might have an excessive tendency to dominate that is perfectly obvious to everyone else but not in the least noticeable—that is "blind"—to himself. Most people have blind areas much larger than they think, a fact that is evident especially in a group where a particular individual's behavior is under the scrutiny of many people. In short, my blind area is what other people know about me that I do not know about myself.

The hidden area (area 3) represents the behavior and motivation that is open to self but kept away from others. This quadrant is sometimes referred to as the "hidden agenda." For example, a person in a committee meeting might offhandedly focus attention on a particular project that he knows is embarrassing to one of the other committee members. Or perhaps a worker might want a particular assignment from his supervisor that he knows will make him look great and allow him to manipulate his way to success without his boss's knowledge of his motives. Or perhaps someone is offended by a rude remark made by someone else, but keeps his resentment to himself. In other words, the hidden area includes anything that you know about yourself that you withhold from others.

A simple way of differentiating the open area from the hidden area is to think of as open those things that are "on top of the table" and as hidden those behaviors motivated by issues "under the table." Therefore, the hidden area is what I know about myself that I do not want others to know.

The area of unknown activity (quadrant 4) is where motivation and behavior are known by neither self nor others. This quadrant obviously does exist, because an individual and persons with whom he is associated discover from time to time "new" motives and behaviors that were present all the time. For example, a person might surprise himself and others by taking charge during a critical time and reconciling warring factions in a group. Although no one before that time was able to see him as a peacemaker (including him), the potential for this activity was always there. In other words, the unknown area is what neither I nor others know about myself.

When a person joins a completely new group or first meets another person, the area of open, shared activity (quadrant one) is extremely small. In this sort of interaction people tend to behave in a relatively polite and superficial manner. Social convention provides a pattern for getting acquainted and forbids a person to act too friendly too soon or reveal too much.

A person who has difficulty relating to others might be described by the same window of awareness. For example, an overly shy person might have difficulty developing a large open area (quadrant 1) even after spending a great deal of time with a group or another individual. Sometimes this type of person might try to hide behind a flurry of words, but allow very little of himself to become available to or known by others.

The window of a person who is becoming actualized is charac-

Johari Window of a Person in a New Situation

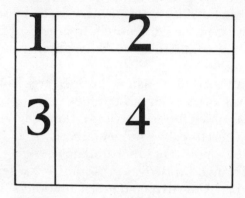

terized by a large open area. It takes substantial psychological and spiritual resources to gradually reduce and wall off the blind, hidden, and unknown quadrants. The larger the open area, the closer to self-realization an individual is in meeting his needs, utilizing his abilities, expressing his interests, and at the same time, making himself more available to others.

Johari Window of an Actualized Person

$$
\begin{array}{|c|c|}
\hline
1 & 2 \\
\hline
3 & 4 \\
\hline
\end{array}
$$

It is incorrect to think that a large open area illustrates extroversion, gregariousness, or sociability. The emphasis is on personal freedom and working with and enjoying others.

The attitude of other people toward the new or shy individual is often suspicion and distrust. On the other hand, the attitude toward the actualized person tends to be acceptance and understanding. Whether between peer associates or supervisor and subordinate, the relationship that fosters openness and self-actualization will result in greater understanding, cooperation, and freedom of activity than any other type of relationship. Those relationships marked by less openness, that remain locked into the early stages of relating, are characterized by suspicion, distrust, tension, anxiety, and gossip.

Persons accustomed to operating with a limited area of openness initially find it painful to "enlarge" that quadrant, but such a change does result in better relationships. One example of this is when two individuals have had a quarrel that revealed previously blind, hidden, or unknown areas, thus resulting in better understanding and a stronger relationship. In groups, when several people are under great tension and stress, they tend to reveal more of themselves to others who are experiencing the same things. A cohesive bond thus develops between those who have suffered together.

With this understanding of the personal window of awareness, you can draw the window illustrating how you relate to others—and perhaps learn more about yourself. Above all, you must be honest with yourself or this project will reveal nothing worthwhile. First construct the window that illustrates your relationship with your family.

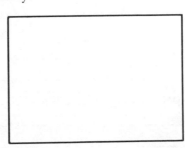

Next illustrate the window that shows how you relate to your friends at church.

Draw the window that illustrates your relationship with your supervisor at the place where you work or your professors and advisers at school.

Are you surprised at any one of the windows you just constructed? List the ways you can improve the proportion of the open area.

1. Family: _____

_____

_____

_____

2. Friends: _____

_____

_____

3. Supervisor or professors: _____

_____

_____

Self-Acceptance

There is a great undiscovered territory in self-acceptance. An individual's acceptance of his own personhood significantly helps his ability to cope with reality.

When someone says "self-acceptance," your first thought is probably concerning the physical body. The physical body is the "frame" for the "picture"—the house of the true self or soul. There is nothing short of plastic surgery that will change physical appearance. Physical attractiveness between individuals is usually determined by factors such as body build, height, weight, skin color, and distinctive physical features. I have taken this view concerning my physical appearance:

> I know that my face ain't no star.
> But I don't mind it,
> I am behind it;
> The ones in front get the jar!

A second major area in which an individual must accept himself is abilities, both physical and mental. Although I am neither a super athlete nor a genius, I have determined that I will do the best I can with what I have in the given time. I have adopted this perspective:

> Twinkle, twinkle superstar,
> Though some said you would not go far.
> You showed them guts; you showed them nerve.
> All through the Lord God whom you serve!

Psalm 139 presents a clear statement concerning how God knows and accepts you. Although you have probably read this passage many times, please relax your mind and very slowly read it once again. Trust the Holy Spirit of God to bear witness to you about who you really are.

O Lord, you have examined my heart and know everything about me. You know when I sit or stand. When far away you know my every thought. You chart the path ahead of me, and tell me where to stop and rest. Every moment, you know where I am. You know what I am going to say before I even say it. You both precede and follow me, and place your hand of blessing on my head.

This is too glorious, too wonderful to believe! I can *never* be lost to your Spirit! I can *never* get away from my God! If I go up to heaven, you are there; if I go down to the place of the dead, you are there. If I ride the morning winds to the farthest oceans, even there your hand will guide me, your strength will support me. If I try to hide in the darkness, the night becomes light around me. For even darkness cannot hide from God; to you the night shines as bright as day. Darkness and light are both alike to you.

You made all the delicate, inner parts of my body, and knit them together in my mother's womb. Thank you for making me so wonderfully complex! It is amazing to think about. Your workmanship is marvelous—and how well I know it. You were there while I was being formed in utter seclusion! You saw me before I was born and scheduled each day of my life before I began to breathe. Every day was recorded in your Book!

How precious it is, Lord, to realize that you are thinking about me constantly! I can't even count how many times a day your thoughts turn towards me. And when I waken in the morning, you are still thinking of me! . . .

Search me, O God, and know my heart; test my thoughts. Point out anything you find in me that makes you sad, and lead me along the path of everlasting life. (TLB)

I believe that as a person becomes more comfortable with his self-identity and builds self-acceptance, he stops trying to make other people conform to what he thinks they should be like. This is a meaningful position because it not only makes him free around others, but frees others to be themselves when in his presence. This is truly when self-acceptance starts making sense.

One of my professors once commented, "If you are smart enough to be aware of feelings of inferiority, you are smart enough to eliminate them!" When you feel inferior about your value and dignity you are probably mentally equal or superior to others but neurotically inferior. This happens when you compare your total self to one or two special virtues of other people. If you have a negative self-concept, whether or not there is a reason, it will be reflected in your attitudes and dealings with yourself and others.

Feelings of inferiority are usually caused by some of the following reasons:

● Comparing your negative characteristics with other people's positive characteristics

● Being overly impressed with other people's successes

● Being a perfectionist and expecting too much from yourself and others

● Lacking a sense of proportion and balance of the components of life

● Allowing fear of failure to prevent you from trying to achieve or relate

● Having a poor sense of humor and ability to laugh at yourself at times

There are positive ways to change feelings of inferiority. First, take direct action toward changing whatever is wrong. If you can do something to change matters, do it! Second, overcompensate for whatever is lacking. When you have the courage to persist, your shortcomings will often provide a springboard to new success. A third option is to shift emphasis from your problem area to something in which you excel. Finally, if you cannot change the problem or substitute one of your strengths, then accept your limitations. However, do not let your limitations get the best of you; you make the best of them. Acknowledge that negative aspects of your personality exist, but do not become obsessed with them. In other words, feelings of inferiority regarding your own value and dignity can be changed or relieved if you only employ the same degree of intelligence to face your problems that you have created them with!

As an individual deals with himself realistically, an important step to understanding and accepting self is to recognize that human nature combines three distinct components into one being. The self is composed of an interacting triad of body, mind (which includes emotion and will), and spirit. Self-acceptance is enhanced when an individual becomes aware of and fosters the growth of each aspect of his personality. Simplistically stated, a human being is three components in one: a body, which contains a mind, which contains a spirit.

The Three Aspects of the Self

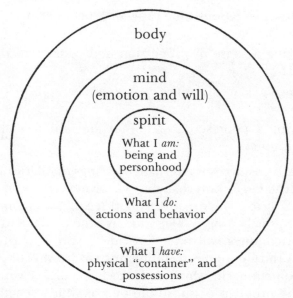

The body is the part of the self that I possess—what I have. My physical body is the "container" for the real me. (I also have physical possessions.) Care of the body promotes health and well-being.

The mind (or emotion and will) is the manifestation of what I do—my actions and behavior. The mind tells the body what to do. Awareness of the needs of the mind will build understanding and healthy attitudes and feelings, and will guide right behavior.

The spirit is the dynamic spark of life that is my being. At the core of human nature is the spirit, which controls the mind. Of course, for the Christian, the health of the spirit is of the greatest importance.

The Real World

Many single adults who are college or seminary students have the when-I-get-out-into-the-real-world syndrome. These people are always dreaming of what they will do or what it will be like when they graduate, get out into the real world, and begin real life. It is rare for a week to pass without my hearing a student in one of my university classes say something about his dreams about the real world. The natural inference from this way of speaking is that life at college or seminary is not real.

Perhaps a better set of labels for college and business is "protected" and "unprotected." The student's world is protected from many of the responsibilities and risks that occur in the business world. (One of my sixth-year college students proudly announced to me one day that "college was the last step before growing up," and he just was not ready to face the cold cruel world.)

The label "unprotected" is relatively accurate for life in the business world. Most single adults are already in the unprotected world of business and they realize that life is real *now*.

At one point in my life, I was guilty of living with my attention focused either five years in the past or ten years in the future. I realized that with my luck, I would probably die before my expectations were fulfilled or Christ would return. Because I negated the present to the past and future I could have lost out altogether, but I determined to commit the past to the Lord, entrust the future to God, and celebrate living in the time I *now* have. Thus, my good todays make some fantastic yesterdays and help me prepare for some wonderful tomorrows.

Here is a personal inventory that you can take to reveal if you are living in the "now" of the real world. Answer these questions honestly.

1. What is the purpose of my life? _____

_____

_____

2. What am I doing? _____

_____

_____

3. How much do I dwell on last year? _____

_____

_____

4. In what ways do I look forward to next week? _____

_____

_____

5. What will I be doing and where will I be five years from now?

_____

_____

_____

6. When I wake up in the morning is my first reaction, "Good morning, God!" or "Good God, morning!"? _____

_____

_____

The responses that you give to these questions will indicate whether you are dwelling in the past, celebrating the present, or dreaming of the future.

Living with Illusions and Disillusionment

In times of loneliness, when your heart is aching and tears are streaming down your face, you often begin thinking, "Why?" A relationship with someone or your concept of faith has crumbled, and you are bitterly disappointed. Why did this happen?

People live in a constant battle with illusions and disillusionment as they search for reality. Treating things or concepts as true when they are not necessarily true is suffering or creating an illusion; disillusionment occurs when the illusion is recognized or uncovered. In other words, when I believe someone is a certain type of person who behaves a particular way and I find out that they have fooled me, my illusion of them is broken and I become disillusioned with them or my ability to understand others.

We have illusions about many aspects of our lives. For example, at one time I thought that professors had all the answers and that physicians could heal anyone. When I learned that professors have unanswered questions and that medicine faces the limits of human knowledge and technology, I became disillusioned with those professions. In another instance, I considered a certain person to be my friend until he ended our relationship and caused me to become disillusioned. I originally believed that God would not permit anything bad to happen in my life. After a tragedy, my faith was shattered.

Disillusionment is the experience of facing a broken illusion about a person, relationship, concept of faith, hope, or idea. The causes for disillusionment are mistaken beliefs, faulty ideas, and unrealistic and unhealthy attitudes. Some illusions are relatively harmless, while some have the potential of being destructive.

For me personally, as an idealist, it is difficult at times to be realistic. (Be careful: a bitter cynic is usually a disillusioned idealist.) However, did my disillusionment truly involve professors, physicians, friends, and God? Or was I actually disillusioned with my illusion—my false impression—of each one of them? In other words, did I really know those people and concepts, or had I made up my mind who and what they were before interacting with them and discovering the facts? When they did not "perform" the way I desired them to or thought they should, was I mistakenly rejecting them rather than rejecting my illusion of them? After a long trail of tears, I realized that I was not facing reality, but was holding tightly to my illusions even when experience proved them false.

Reality is accepting things as they are and not making them be something they are not. Perhaps you have desperately asked yourself the question, "How can I accept the reality of things as they are rather than suffering illusions and then becoming disillusioned?"

First, do not set yourself up for disillusionment. Do not make up your mind about anything or anyone until you have the facts. Do not be too impressed because a person, concept, or thing initially appears to be a certain way. Time will tell. In a humorous yet serious manner I say, "Time either heals all wounds or wounds all heels!" Second, reevaluate how and why you have falsely believed certain things in your world in the past. Was it because you were too idealistic? Do not be afraid to get to know people or situations as they really are. Be open. Third, be flexible. Life does go on. If life gives you a lemon, make lemonade, serve it to your friends, and have a party.

Be brave and answer the following questions honestly.

1. In the past, how have I created or suffered illusions? _____

_____

_____

2. How do I set myself up for disillusionment?   _____

_____

_____

3. Am I really disillusioned with some things and relationships or am I disillusioned with my illusions—my false ideas—of them? In what ways am I disillusioned with my illusions? _____

_____

_____

4. In what manner do I handle my disillusionment?   _____

_____

_____

5. Because of these new insights into my behavior, how can I realistically relate better to others? _____

_____

Chapter Two
RELATIONSHIPS

Relationships
with Others

Communicating and relating are basic human imperatives. Relationships are inevitable! It is impossible to avoid communicating and relating because it is impossible to avoid people. It seems that each day more and more people are pressed together in compact areas of metropolitan living. One day this week as you raced to work or school you probably noticed a new apartment complex, dormitory, or suburban development.

The increased specialization of professional roles has increased interdependence between people. Personally and professionally an individual therefore comes in contact with a great number of people on a daily basis. With so many people around, every person needs to learn how to adequately communicate and relate.

When a person is with other people and they are aware of his presence, it is impossible for the group to avoid responding to one another. Even no response is actually a response of rejection. It is important to realize that a person apparently trying to avoid communicating or relating is often communicating quite a bit. These unspoken communications, which usually reflect negatively upon the person they are directed toward, might cause more of an impact than something said with words. A person's body language, facial expressions, and vocal tone around another person tell a great deal about the relationship.

One way of achieving meaningful relationships is to overcome potential barriers and problems. Barriers and breakdowns in communication and relationships arise from multiple factors. Some of these include *philosophical assumptions.* Attitudes, prejudices, and biases are "filters" that new information must pass through as an individual builds understanding regarding a concept or relationship. Many times people have differences because of the ways they perceive life. After all, a person sees things not as *they* are but as *he* is! In other words, what a person thinks or says about another probably tells more about himself than it does about that other person.

Alienation is another factor in communication breakdown. The common usage of the word "alienation" usually refers to an estrangement or withdrawal of one person from other people with whom he would ordinarily be expected to associate. Alienation is not simple disagreement with another person; it refers to withdrawal from interaction. In this sense, an individual can become alienated from a person or group—spouse, friend, children, supervisor, work colleagues, or social groups—when he concludes that attempts to relate are pointless. Many times one can get into double binds with people. Regardless of what one does or says one is at fault: wrong if I "do" and wrong if I "don't."

One of the strongest barriers to healthy relationships is *distrust.* If a person thinks that another individual is trustworthy then he will have little problem relating to that individual. If he is suspicious about that person, however, there will be relational barriers. Sometimes the problem of questionable trust in a relationship is not warranted, but on the other hand a broken confidence or untrue comment can reduce credibility and cause barriers and breakdowns in communication and the relationship.

Guilt, the feeling of having committed a breach of conduct, often chokes communication. Human nature dictates that when a person thinks someone is holding something against him he will feel guilty and hostile toward that someone. Guilt also occurs when a person does not meet what he expects of himself or what others expect of him. Therefore, when a person thinks or knows that another individual considers something he has done to be "below standard," he will feel guilt, which will break down communication with that individual.

The barrier that is potentially most harmful to an individual's self-esteem is *rejection.* Everyone has experienced a time when someone refused to acknowledge or relate to him. Rejection of this sort presents an almost insurmountable barrier to communication. In the most profound sense, rejection can be described as "psychological murder," when an individual denies another person's existence. To say that rejection is a painful experience is a gross understatement. Most people would rather risk the comfort of only mild degrees of rejection than to disclose themselves fully and be severely hurt by total rejection. Therefore they do not open up enough to ever know true acceptance. They have preprogrammed themselves for rejection.

Alternatives for Building or Dissolving Relationships

People are constantly analyzing, evaluating, and changing their relationships with others. Relationships are evaluated most of the time by comparing the rewards received against the costs incurred. After an initial contact is made between two people the survival of the relationship will depend upon the cost-reward ratio. If either one or both of the people involved determine that the cost-reward level is not optimum, the intensity of the relationship will be changed. There are several alternatives that can be taken to change the intensity of a relationship, or continue it as it is, depending upon the costs and rewards involved.

Perhaps the most obvious possible action for two people in a relationship to take is to continue the status quo based on relative satisfaction with the relationship as it currently exists. In this situation there are no real issues or pressures that need to be handled to permit the relationship to continue as it is. The people in the relationship do not apply any pressure to significantly change anything concerning their communicating and relating. Maintaining the status quo is the typical response to a surface relationship that one feels no desire to change.

The alternative that is available for two people who are growing together is to increase the intensity of relating and move toward a more meaningful relationship. A relationship moves from nonintimate to intimate when both persons realize their capacity to become closer. As persons respond favorably to one another their psychological distance will be reduced and the potential for enjoyable communication enhanced. They will expect their relationship to become more meaningful as time goes along. By building relationships in this way, people increase involvement and intensify feelings.

As relationships continue to grow, the people involved will determine the level of commitment desired. Commitment is the gauge that determines degrees of sharing—from sharing material things to sharing lives in marriage.

If a relationship begins to decay, however, the partners usually show an inclination toward reducing involvement or moving from intimate status to nonintimate relating. This is accomplished through several changes. The first is an increase in physical distance between the partners and a decrease in amount of time spent together. The number of encounters will decrease and the length of time for each will become shorter. Another change is the reduction of personal contact: less personal information will be discussed, nonverbal responses will decrease (moving to indirect eye contact and cooler vocal tone), and favors will rarely be requested or given. The final step in reducing involvement in a relationship often takes the form of a farewell speech given by one or both parties as they end intimate connections and acknowledge a more nonintimate relationship.

If the costs of a relationship exceed the rewards even after a reduction of intimacy, the partners have the option of ending the relationship totally. However, the cliché "breaking up is hard to do" is profoundly true, and if only one person wants out, terminating a relationship is even more difficult. Some people will degenerate to the "fifty ways to leave your lover" method of making things so intolerable that the other person will demand termination of the relationship. Despite the difficulties involved, it is obvious that simple acquaintances can terminate a relationship with greater ease than intimates.

Brokenness to Wholeness

When any type of relationship—friendship, dating, engagement, or marriage—is broken, healing is required. Many times a broken relationship can be viewed as a call to personal wholeness. There are a number of key stages that transpire in the process of growth from brokenness to wholeness.

Shock results from realization of the fact that the relationship has actually disintegrated. The person says, "I cannot believe that this relationship really ended. I saw some possible warnings, and knew that it could happen. But now it *has* happened! What does this mean?" He feels like his world is destroyed because what he once feared could happen is now coming to pass.

The idea that the relationship might have ended because of personal shortcomings gives rise to feelings of *inadequacy*. As shock starts wearing away, the partner of a broken relationship asks himself some questions. "How did this happen? Why did this occur in my life?" He feels devastated, and hurts emotionally. He looks at his situation and says, "I am not good. Nothing is right with me. No one loves me." Then deep introspection begins to further the downward spiral.

Feelings of inadequacy and personal dissatisfaction swell into *rejection of self,* and result in real or false guilt. The former partner starts feeling guilty because of inadequacies that might have contributed to breaking the relationship. False guilt occurs when the individual takes on total responsibility for problems and blames only himself for everything that is wrong. The usual signpost of false guilt is a preoccupation with the insignificant. The individual says, "If I had only done *that* differently. If I had folded his socks differently. If I had only washed the car more often."

Often there is a feeling of real guilt. The partner might not have conducted himself appropriately or might have disobeyed scriptural guidelines for relationships. In other words, he might have committed an infraction that caused the relationship to end. This kind of real guilt must be dealt with in an appropriate manner.

When a person involved in a broken relationship understands whether his guilt is false or real, then he will have some cues for how to deal with it. When he is falsely rejecting himself he usually takes pleasure in "barbecuing self." He becomes his worst enemy, telling everyone what a "turkey" he is and agreeing with everything negative mentioned concerning him. He actually starts believing and acting like he has no value or dignity. Then he serves "barbecued self" at a "pity party" to celebrate his sorrow.

Despite the trouble and pain, there is usually a deep *hope* that the relationship can be salvaged. Sometimes the problems in relationships can be reconciled, sometimes not. Usually during the stage of hope, unrealistic promises—to self and the partner— are made and easily forgotten.

It is possible that the relationship will be reconciled and that the partners will experience new beginnings toward wholeness together. But if this does not occur, the individual must *accept the reality* that the relationship is terminated and that they will not get back together. In some circumstances people do not have the ability or desire to reconcile. Perhaps pride or closed-mindedness on one or both parts prohibits restoration. When this reality "moves in like a freight train," the former partner must admit that, regardless of how hard he tried, the relationship is over.

Often the hurt caused by the dissolution of a relationship causes the injured person to seek *revenge*—to try to get even with the person who hurt him. He says, "I will get even with that sucker! He will wish he had never hurt me." He then takes every possible opportunity to make the "ex" pay for all his personal devastation. Some Christians even enjoy seeking revenge. It feels good to get even—that is, it feels good until the revenge boomerangs. When a person seeks revenge, it usually returns in multiplied proportions.

After the former partner has been emotionally wounded, he often creates protective devices—walls and defenses of emotional distance—to keep from becoming more devastated. He says, "I can get along in my world without that person. I am never going to let anyone hurt me again." When an individual surrounds himself with protective walls of his own making, he shuts himself in as well, depriving himself of relationships with others. It is possible for him to build walls so high that he can neither get out nor let anyone else in.

Defenses usually cause a person to become excessively dependent on himself. Independence is great, but an overdose can be quite unhealthy. The person develops the attitude, "It's God and me. We will conquer the world. Get out of our way!" It is tragic that some people never adjust beyond this point, and never seek a deep and rewarding relationship again.

On the other hand, a former partner of a broken relationship who fosters healthy attitudes toward his problems will gradually come to an *acceptance* of his loss and a *resolution* to live with that loss. The key word is not "solution," it is "resolution"—feelings may be soothed, circumstances cleared up, and events worked out. He does not necessarily "get over" his loss, he learns to live with it.

If a person experiences a broken relationship, the best way for him to resolve or even solve it is to *forgive.* The response to this statement, however, is often "I do not want to forgive." How does a hurt or offended person forgive?

Sometimes the most important thing is to pray for willingness, the true desire to be forgiving. Remember that anything that has to do with thoughts or feelings is probably temporary: if a person just thinks he wants to be forgiving, then he might change his mind; if he only feels that he wants to forgive, then those feelings might change. It is by an act of the will, on the other hand, that true forgiveness occurs. In other words, commitment to God to let him carry out the transaction of forgiveness and openness to him will produce the true spirit of forgiveness: "Lord God, I trust your Spirit to bear witness to my spirit and change the thoughts of my mind and feelings of my heart. You give me the willpower to forgive. Create in me a forgiving response." Something remarkable will happen within the person who prays to forgive with this attitude. He will open himself to a miraculous healing process of the Lord God in his life.

Forgiving is not easy for some people, but the alternative is frustration and interaction in the negative stages of brokenness. A broken relationship is certainly never planned or desired; but as eggs cannot be unscrambled, a broken relationship cannot be unbroken after the fact. When it comes to a broken relationship, to live is to forgive and to forgive is to live.

The final step for the partner of a dissolved relationship is to *release* the other person. He must take this position: "You are free to go and live without me. I am free to go and live without you." As he releases the other person from himself and himself from the other person, he will find a new freedom to begin again. The Lord God will then be free to direct the paths of both people.

Dating and Marriage

Many single people dread dating, marriage, and the possibility of divorce more than any other aspect of singleness and relating. However, we must go beyond the stereotypes many people have concerning singles. "Spinster," "bachelor," "widow," "widower," and "divorcée" are harsh and hurtful words. Behind these stereotypes are individual needs—regardless of the reason for singleness. We must realize that singles stand as individuals, not as halves or potential partners of pair groups.

There are some specific guidelines for the single adult concerning dating. God places these restrictions on the relationships of singles as well as married people in Matthew and 1 Corinthians 7.

First, there is to be no sex outside of marriage. Scripture labels sex outside marriage as fornication for the single and adultery for the married person.

The Scripture also forbids "seeking." The married person should not seek to be free from his spouse; the single should avoid seeking a mate by traditional secular methods. Some people are desperately searching for a mate and will marry the first person who will say yes. However, God wants the privilege of bringing the right person into the single's life at precisely the right time under the right circumstances. One example of a relationship instituted by God is that of Isaac and Rebecca, which is recorded in the Old Testament.

Marriage is certainly not wrong, but the point to remember is that self-seeking can keep any person from having God's best. Profound truth is expressed in the thought that God gives his very best to those who leave the choice to him. In other words, singles should not worry about finding someone to marry, but should relax and trust God to institute and build relationships at the right time. The single who finds someone to marry might do so before God brings the best person to him!

Christians have the responsibility to yield to the Lord God and to conduct themselves properly concerning their life-style and objectives. One important area that the yielded Christian should be obedient in is the choice of associates and friends. If I want to catch a catfish, I go where the catfish are; if I want to catch a bass, I go where there are bass. If I want to find good Christian friends, I should go where Christians gather. The kind of places a person frequents will determine the kind of people he finds.

There are added dimensions to the dating problems of the widow, widower, and divorced person. (Some people use the term "dating again" to describe the unique problems of this group.) If a "single again" feels that remarriage is within God's plan, he or she should take some precautions. In the first place, it is healthy to rethink marriage before thinking remarriage. A healing process should precede remarriage. Commitment is the cement for marriage, and any marriage bonded with poor cement is bound to crack.

It is also important for the "single again," especially the divorced person, to say a healthy "good-bye" to the past before he tries to say "hello" to another relationship. If a person compares new relationships to old ones, he will be inviting trouble. Some people destroy new relationships because they try to hold on to the past rather than grow in the present.

On a spiritual plane, the person considering remarriage must come to a scriptural understanding of sin, grace, forgiveness, and reconciliation. Unless the process of a renewed relationship with Jesus is completed, you will short-circuit the new human relationship with guilt from mistakes that have happened in the past. An important corollary to the renewed spiritual relationship is the need to realize that no human being can bring ultimate happiness or success. These feelings come from being rightly related to the Lord God. Remember: personal happiness is a by-product, not a goal!

The dread of the tension points of singleness—dating, marriage, and divorce—can be diminished through an understanding of the definition of "love," a word that is often misused. In the English language there is only one word to define feelings of affection for family, friends, mate, or God. In the Greek language, however, there are four words to convey the dimensions of love.

The first type is *storge* or love for family members. It is basically a love of blood relatives. The next kind of love is that of *phileo* which is used to describe the love of a friend. There is a *phileo*-love for friends in multiple levels from acquaintances to committed friendships. *Eros* is the love of a spouse. An *eros*-love is a continuous, growing, dynamic love which becomes more meaningful as time goes along. For those whom the Lord has called into marriage, *eros* is ordained by and pleasing to God. The most complete of all love is *agape*. This is the divine love of God for all people.

Love is either conditional or unconditional. I either give conditions to my love for you or I do not. To the extent that I place conditions on my love, I do not really love you. I am not offering you the gift of my love, I am offering an "exchange." *True* love in any category is unconditional and must always be a free gift. Whether in friendship or marriage, this is what relating is all about. I extend my unconditional love to you and you respond with the gift of your unconditional love to me!

Many marriage manuals deal mostly with trivia, but the Scripture gives real answers. In Genesis 2:18–25 and Ephesians 5, marriage is spoken of as a mystery. In biblical terms a mystery can be understood only by the revelation of God. Therefore, we are never going to understand what makes a good marriage until we understand what the Bible says, and let it explain the mystery from God's viewpoint.

One of my friends says that marriage does not so much involve finding the right person as it does *being* the right person. Finding is not a difficult process when a person pays attention to being the person God wants him to be.

Scripture relates that there are three components in a good marriage. The first, and most important, is the Lord God. A good marriage relationship involves a triangle of God, man, and woman. Two of my friends had engraved inside their wedding rings the statement, "We Three." It is God who ordained marriage, who brings a man and woman together, and God's presence is necessary for the relationship to grow.

Second, a responsible man is required. God saw that it was not good for man to be alone in the Garden of Eden, so he brought Eve to Adam. The man then became responsible for the leadership of the godly marriage. Leadership does not involve being a dictator or bully, but is demonstrated by responsibility even to the point of self-sacrifice. For the marriage to be healthy, the man has to be the leader in cultivating the relationship.

Third, the relationship needs a virtuous and cooperative woman. She is co-worker with the man in marriage. The godly wife, who possesses the virtues described in Proverbs 31:10–31, is far more valuable than riches, because she knows the Lord God and works with her husband.

The man and wife must leave other family members and cleave to one another. Marriage requires resolve to "stick to it" and time to become all it is meant to be. There is a gradual process involved in marriage becoming what God wants it to be. A good marriage does not instantly happen.

Proverb 31:30
Favor is deceitful and beauty is Vain, but a ~~woman~~ that feareth the Lord, she shall be Praised!

Chapter Three
REVELATION

Tuning in to the
Inner Self

For a person to accept himself as a physical, emotional, and spiritual being, it is important for him to understand his personality temperaments. Have you ever heard anyone say, "That's the way I am; I cannot help it?" Usually a statement like that is a cop out to force others to adjust to his ways rather than for him to change his behavior. Sometimes there is some truth to such a claim.

Every human personality is made up of a combination of characteristics. The classic Greek and Roman philosophers, as well as contemporary writers, have categorized these characteristics into temperaments or personality types. Hippocrates, a Greek philosopher and physician, was the first to give some attention to this field, four hundred years before the time of Christ. Roman thinkers continued to follow and develop Greek ideas about personality. In the late 1700s, the German philosopher Immanuel Kant was influential in popularizing a revised theory of temperaments in Europe. Contemporary author Tim

45

LaHaye has familiarized America with the classic concepts of the four personality temperaments.

According to the theory, most people are dominated by characteristics of one temperament and are strongly influenced by traits in a second or third type. A study of the four temperaments will enable you to examine yourself and determine your strengths and weaknesses.

There are several things that you should keep in mind as you try to determine the principal temperament that characterizes yourself or others. One of the most important points is that no one person is entirely described by just one temperament, although he might be in one predominant category. There is also real danger in presenting the four personality types, because some people are tempted to become amateur psychologists, analyzing everyone they meet along the framework of "What type is he?"

This outline of the temperaments is primarily for self-analysis. As a by-product of your analysis you should become more understanding of the strengths and weaknesses of others and become more patient and loving. Remember that these are only general classifications.

The person of *sanguine* temperament is an extroverted optimist. He is lively, emotionally positive and warm, by nature friendly and personable. He is happy, enjoys entertaining people, and is at his best when he is the life of the party. The sanguine is a good salesman, since he is never at a loss for words. He is also often successful as an entertainer, social worker, actor, or speaker. Therefore, the people with sanguine temperament significantly enrich the world.

There are possible weaknesses as well as strengths in each temperament, and the sanguine is no exception. He is often restless, disorganized, impractical, and egotistical. His noisy mannerisms make him appear more confident than he really is, and sometimes cause the envy of people who are less extroverted. The special spiritual needs of the sanguine person are self-control, long-suffering, faith, peace, and goodness.

The apostle Peter is probably the most famous sanguine in the Bible. In contemporary days Grady Nutt and Jerry Clower are classic examples of this personality temperament.

The *melancholy* person is generally an introverted pessimist. He is extremely selective, analytical, and thorough concerning life. Being a deep thinker, his idealism tends to exaggerate the negative. Therefore, he is a perfectionist with a sensitive, emotional nature who finds a great deal of meaning in life from some form of personal sacrifice. He is a faithful friend and has a deep appreciation for aesthetics.

Several philosophers have concluded that the melancholy temperament has the greatest strengths of the four types. However, this positive potential is usually accompanied by some of the largest potential weaknesses. He can be subject to weaknesses such as moodiness, self-centeredness, inflexibility, and a critical or vengeful disposition. If the melancholiac is dominated by his weaknesses, he can become a neurotic hypochondriac who neither enjoys himself nor is enjoyed by others. If a person of melancholy temperament sees two people talking, he assumes that they are saying something bad about him. (The sanguine in the same situation assumes they are admiring him.)

Many great artists, educators, inventors, geniuses and musicians were melancholy. In biblical times, Moses and the apostle John are two of the outstanding melancholy personalities. In modern times, some of the most famous melancholy people are W. A. Criswell, Jack Taylor, Billy Graham, Manley Beasley, and Peter Lord.

The *choleric* temperament is best illustrated by the strong-willed, hard-driving person. The choleric person has a quick, active, and practical nature. He is usually self-sufficient and independent and sets extremely high goals that he works tirelessly to achieve. Decisions for himself and others are easy for him to make. Since he thrives on activity, adversities only serve as encouragement for him.

On the bad side, the choleric person does not sympathize with or show much compassion toward others. He tends to use people for his own purposes and then ignores them when their usefulness has ended. His hard-driving disposition sometimes causes him to be opportunistic.

Despite these negative characteristics, there are positive leadership traits. Most of the world's great leaders, executives, idea men, and producers have been cholerics.

The greatest spiritual needs of the choleric person include gentleness, meekness, goodness, and long-suffering. Yet some people with this temperament have yielded to the Lord God and have become powerful Christian leaders. Among Bible characters, the apostle Paul is most often mentioned. In recent times, people like James Robison, Richard Jackson, and Miss Bertha Smith stand out as notable cholerics.

The slow, good natured person probably has a *phlegmatic* temperament. He is calm, cool, well-balanced, and easygoing and avoids as much involvement as is possible. His life is happy, pleasant, and generally uneventful. The phlegmatic person never gets ruffled or angry, regardless of circumstances, and seldom laughs. He keeps his own emotions under control, but he enjoys a dry sense of humor and can keep people in stitches without ever cracking a smile. He is a big teaser who delights in poking fun at other temperaments.

A person of phlegmatic temperament makes a good accountant, diplomat, scientist, teacher, leader, or technician. Abraham is a biblical example of the classic phlegmatic temperament. Tom Landry, Vance Havner, Ron Dunn, and Bill Gothard are some modern phlegmatics.

Personality temperament is the raw material from which actions and behavior are formed. There are several fundamental behavioral profiles that modify basic temperament, emphasizing characteristics or modes of manipulation common to some people. An understanding of these behavior profiles will help deepen your knowledge of yourself and how you relate to others.[2]

The *dictator* exaggerates his strengths in order to dominate and control people. Quoting authorities and giving orders are the dictator's pleasure. Variations of the dictator include the "boss," "rank-puller," "godfather," and "God's junior partner."

The *weakling,* often the dictator's victim, exhibits behavior directly opposite from the dictator. The weakling tries to develop skills to cope with the dictator and emphasizes his sensitivity and passive silence. Different forms the weakling takes are the "confused" or "spacy" person, "worrier," and "withdrawer."

The *calculator* tries to control other people by outwitting and deceiving them and lying to them. Variations of the calculator are the "poker player," "con artist," "blackmailer," and "seducer."

The *clinging vine* exaggerates his dependence and behaves much the opposite of the calculator. He wants to be taken care of, led around, and pampered. He is glad to let others do his work for him. Several alternative manifestations of the clinging vine include the "parasite," "helpless" person, "hypochondriac," "crier," and "baby."

The *bully* talks and acts aggressively and cruelly. He loves to control other people by implied or direct threats; pushing people around is a favorite game. Behavior variations of the bully are the "tough guy," "threatener," "nagger," and "humiliator."

The *nice guy* kills everybody with kindness. At times the nice guy will almost make you sick of niceness when you are around him because he seems more sugar-coated than real. Love and caring are of course key positive qualities, but the nice guy overemphasizes them to the point that everyone sees they are false. There are several variations of the nice guy, such as the "pleaser," "nonoffender," and "goody-goody."

The *judge* delights in criticism, does not trust anyone, and blames whomever he can. Often holding resentment, the judge is slow to forgive. Specific forms of the judge are the "convictor," "blamer," and "know-it-all."

The *protector* exaggerates support in a manner directly opposite to the judge. The protector is oversympathetic, nonjudgmental, and uncritical; he spoils others. He will not let the people he is protecting stand up for themselves and grow up. Variations of the protector are the "helper," "martyr," and "defender."

Many people say, "My personality temperament and behavior patterns hinder me." They get themselves locked in to their hang-ups and try to use them to explain why they cannot live for God. But the Christian can live for God if he chooses to!

The real reason many people do not live for God is due to their ignorance of the Word or their disobedience. The more a person understands about his temperament and behavior, the more he should desire to give himself to God. As he makes himself available to God and searches the Scripture for guidelines, the joy of victory will follow.

James 4:7-8 gives some meaningful insights for tuning into the inner self. First, give yourself humbly to God. Giving yourself to God requires action on your part. It is a powerfully humbling experience for an unholy person to approach the holy and righteous Lord God Almighty!

Second, resist the devil so that he will flee from you. Realize that you are involved in spiritual warfare; be conscious of the enemy that you are battling. Put on the whole armor of God against the devil. The appropriate way to meet the devil is with the Word of God. Each time Jesus was tempted by the devil, he always met the confrontation by quoting the Word.

Third, draw close to God so that he will draw close to you. Have you ever noticed that as you get closer to someone you love, they draw closer to you? This is much more true with God. He wants to be close to us, but we often keep him away simply by not attending to our part of the relationship. The Christian draws close to God by cleansing his inner life—his heart—and outer relationships—his hands.

Fourth, wash your hands of sin. It is impossible for a sinful human to properly fellowship with the holy God. It is the Christian's responsibility to confess all known sin in his life to God. God will then forgive him and cleanse him from all unrighteousness. The person with a cleansed heart and mind must then determine to stop deliberately sinning.

Fifth, fill your heart with God alone to be pure and true. After a person's heart is cleansed, he must put the Word of God to work.

Take God at his word, meditate, and put into practice what he reveals to you through the Scripture.

Pulling off
the Mask

Although modern society places a great emphasis on "being real," most people actually play roles and wear masks in order to disguise their true selves. The amount a person will risk in self-disclosure depends partially on his successes or failures in the past. If past risks promoted growth in self and relationships, he will probably have positive attitudes about revealing himself in the present and future. On the other hand, if the risks he took resulted in others using the revealed information to hurt him, he will be cautious and reluctant to disclose his true self. Pulling off the mask and disclosing the self involve many elements of risk.

Self-disclosure is the process by which a person intentionally and unintentionally reveals information about himself. Sometimes he knows exactly what he is telling about himself; at other times, he does not. The individual learns at an early age that as the information disclosed to others about self becomes more intimate, the amount of pain they can inflict upon him increases. He cannot have any way of really knowing the motives of others unless he asks, but he has no right to ask others to disclose unless he is willing to disclose himself. (A further problem is the fact that most people are not willing to reveal their true motives even when asked.)

Self-disclosure is a way of tuning in to and understanding oneself. In other words, a person can only learn about himself as he tells others who he is.

When a person tells others about himself, he runs the risk of rejection, ego deflation, or negative communication. This might be the reason that self-disclosure is usually so shallow. Most people have deep fears of telling others who they really are; if their disclosure is rejected, then they do not know what to do!

The real question for an individual is not whether to disclose, but *when* to disclose! The person who indiscriminately reveals himself to others will eventually be hurt, but the individual who looks for opportunities for self-disclosure will both grow and save himself from unnecessary pain. The key is to evaluate the capacity and desire to share with particular people and gradually risk trust, stepping out on faith.

The following statement was written anonymously. Most people can easily identify with the writer.

Don't be fooled by me.
Don't be fooled by the face I wear.
For I wear a mask. I wear a thousand masks,
    masks that I'm afraid to take off
    and none of them are me.

Pretending is an art that's second nature with me
But don't be fooled, for God's sake don't be fooled.
I give you the impression that I'm secure
That all is sunny and unruffled with me
        within as well as without
        that confidence is my name
        and coolness my game,
        and the water's calm
        and I'm in command,
        and that I need no one.
But don't believe me. Please!
My surface might be smooth but my surface is my mask—
My ever-varying and ever-concealing mask.
Beneath lies no smugness, no complacence.
Beneath dwells the real me in confusion, in fear, in aloneness.
    But I hide this;
    I don't want anybody to know it.
    I panic at the thought of my weaknesses
    and fear exposing them.
That's why I frantically create my masks to hide behind.
They're nonchalant, sophisticated façades to help me pretend,
To shield me from the glance that knows.
But such a glance is precisely my salvation,
        my only salvation,
        and I know it.
That is, if it's followed by acceptance, if it's followed by love.

It's the only thing that can liberate me from myself
    from my own self-built prison walls
    from the barriers that I so painstakingly erect.
That glance is the only thing that assures me
    of what I can't assure myself
    that I'm really worth something.

But I don't tell you this.
    I don't dare.
    I'm afraid to.

I'm afraid you'll think less of me, that you'll laugh—
    and your laugh would kill me.
I'm afraid that deep down I'm nothing, that I'm just no good
    and you will see this
    and reject me.
So I play my game, my desperate, pretending game;
With a façade of assurance without
And a trembling child within
So begins the parade of masks
The glittering but empty parade of masks,
and my life becomes a front.
I idly chatter to you in suave tones of surface talk.
I tell you everything that's nothing
And nothing of what's everything, of what's crying within me.
So when I'm going through my routine
Do not be fooled by what I'm saying.
Please listen carefully and try to hear
    what I'm *not* saying.
Hear what I'd like to say
    but what I cannot say.

I dislike hiding.
    Honestly.
I dislike the superficial game I'm playing—
    the superficial phony game.
I'd really like to be genuine
    and spontaneous
    and me.
But I need your help, your hand to hold;
Even though my masks would tell you otherwise.

It will not be easy for you.

Long-felt inadequacies make my defenses strong.
The nearer you approach me
The blinder I may strike back.
Despite what books say of men, I am irrational;
I fight against the very thing that I cry out for.

You wonder who I am?
You shouldn't—
        for I am every man
        and every woman
        who wears a mask.
Don't be fooled by me.
At least not by the face I wear.

As you read this statement, did you have the feeling that
someone had photographed your thoughts?

Another major problem concerning masks and relating to
other people is stereotypes. Stereotypes are preconceived opinions of certain groups of people based on rumors, folk tales, and
other ill-conceived sources of information. Stereotypes are
instant mental images by which individuals classify people; they
often reflect rather automatic and robotlike perceptions of
others. Several typical stereotypes follow these lines: "Singles are
all either swingers or perverts." "Football players are all dumb."
"Divorcées are easy catches." *not this one!*

It is obvious that stereotypes can cause a person to be prejudiced against another. When a person is judged on the basis of
tales and hearsay rather than his own identity, others might never
come to know the real person or the relationships that could have
been possible. It is unfortunate, but once a prejudiced stereotype
is allowed to enter an individual's mind, then all encounters with
people who "fit that mold" are perceived in light of that
prejudice.

Unconfusing Religion

The majority of people in the world claim some religious
connection, yet there is a distinct difference between being

affiliated with a religion and having a personal relationship with Jesus Christ! Of all the world's religious leaders, Jesus Christ is the only one who has fulfilled his claims.

Even among Christians, there are several immature, inadequate, or even unscriptural concepts about who God really is. Some perceive God as a "slot machine in the sky," into which one puts offering money, pulls the prayer lever, and awaits the payoff. Others view God as a giant computer that people feed their problems into for automatic answers. Spiritual things are treated like a data system: punch the problem card, run it through the computer, and "the machine" will kick out answers at church.

Another inadequate concept of God is that he is a spiritual Santa Claus with a sack full of gifts to give to those who have been good. The assumption is that if a person lives right, then only good things will happen to him.

One of the most damaging concepts that people have about God portrays him as a policeman who keeps unruly humans in line. They believe God is watching and hoping they will mess up so he can crack them over the head with a club.

Perhaps the most common misconception people have is that God is a formal Sunday event. In other words, God is only to be worshiped through ritual and form, organ music and sermons.

It is imperative that Christians have a scriptural concept of God. It is impossible to have a healthy relationship with God without having a scriptural understanding of who he is! An inadequate concept of God will bring about a wrong response to him; a distorted idea will cause a distorted relationship with him. On the other hand, a scriptural idea of God will build a healthy relationship with him.

Scripture reveals God as the trinity of Father, Son, and Spirit. Throughout time, God has been revealing himself, and Scripture gives a progressive revelation of his nature.

The first expression of God is God the Father: the creator, ruler, and sustainer of the universe and every person in it— including me and you! In the Bible, God gradually revealed himself by sharing his names with his people: *Elohim,* "the supreme, all powerful God"; *El Shaddai,* "the Almighty God"; *Jehovah-Jireh,* "the Provider"; *Jehovah,* "Redeemer and Lord"; *Jehovah-Rophe,* "the Healer"; *Jehovah-Nissi,* "the Banner of Victory"; *Jehovah-Shalom,* "Our Peace"; *Jehovah-Rohi,* "Our Shepherd"; and *Jehovah-Shammah,* "Our God Who Dwells with Us." Therefore, God the Father loves us so much that he not only gave us life, but also provides for us.

The second aspect of God is God the Son: Jesus Christ, who is Savior and Lord of those who trust him. The greatest revelation of God is given through Jesus, who came to tell human beings about the Father in heaven. Even greater than that, Jesus came to provide the way for people to be reunited with the Father. God the Father is the example of what a good father is like; Jesus is the example of what a good child is like.

The third expression of God is God the Spirit, the one who illuminates the Scripture and enables ordinary humans to perform divine work. Just as holy men of old were inspired to write the Scripture, Christians today must trust the same Spirit of God to illuminate spiritual truths. The Holy Spirit convicts men of their need for Jesus the Savior and Jesus reunites those lost ones with the Father.

In the Christian faith there is a battle between legalism and libertinism. The "carnal" or libertine Christian boasts of his liberty, while the legalist "spiritual" Christian boasts of his slavery to Jesus. (Do not confuse legalism with fundamentalism and libertinism with liberalism.)

Legalists get caught up more with the means of Christianity than the end. Several characteristics of the legalist perspective include rigid responses to varying circumstances and interpretation of the Bible as a rule text. Legalists feel comfortable with a "doing it by the numbers" approach, responding to problems or questions like painting a picture by the numbers. In other words, there is no room for expression or creativity. Some look at the Bible as only a comprehensive rule book. Legalists usually live by the letter of the law rather than the spirit of the law, always giving quick answers to problems by quoting passages of Scripture (whether or not they fit the situation).

A danger of relying on the letter of the law is oversimplification of scriptural truths. Legalists sometimes make superficial judgment of scriptural truths rather than getting the deeper meaning of what God is really saying. Some give easy answers for tough questions from a list of scriptures, reciting solutions without thinking and praying. The tendency is to spiritually cop out, and not really to receive guidance from God for a specific situation. I do not mean to be offensive or judgmental; I simply plead that Christians consider the spirit of the law as well as its letter.

The libertinist view regards the Bible as only a guidebook for freedom. Perhaps the most prominent characteristic of the libertine perspective is that its proponents seem to be "drowning in freedom." The stance is, "Once I am saved I am always saved, so I can do anything I desire." Libertines have the carefree attitude of not caring what others think, and they often explain questionable behavior with the boast that Christians should not care what others think, but should be responsible to God alone. This misses the point of witnessing, because it is not what others think of us that matters, but what they think about God because of us! An example of libertine behavior is David in his adultery (2 Samuel 12:14).

Another problem of the libertine perspective is that it presumes on the grace of God. Libertines seem to have no conscience about sin or even the appearance of sin (1 Thessalonians 5:22). With disregard to God's wishes, the libertine declares, "Since God is good I will do what I desire. He will not care."

Can you see characteristics of legalism or libertinism in your own life? I have described these positions with the hope that you will be able to clarify your personal stance. Perhaps some flaws in your theology have been revealed. If you want truly unconfusing religion, be anchored to the Book and geared to the times!

> (Possibility Thinkers Bible)

However, because by this deed you have given great occasion to the enemies of the Lord to blaspheme, the child also who is born to you shall surely die.

The Word of God
in Everyday Life

When a person's faith comes alive there is a meaningful excitement of seeing God's action—and the work of his Word—in the nitty-gritty of everyday living. This comes from appropriating the Scripture or making it applicable to oneself in the daily routine of good and bad times. Trusting God and obeying the Scripture are the key factors in making the Word of God relevant to daily events.

There are two distinct ways the Word of God can come to have special meaning in everyday life. Biblical scholars use two Greek words, "logos" and "rhema" (both of which are translated by the English word "word"), to describe the action of God through the Scripture in everyday life.

The Word of God as "logos" can speak to the believer who has a problem by providing specific answers to the current needs. The believer in a problem situation can call to mind a Scripture passage that particularly discusses his problem and depend on God to care for him as the Bible promises.

If a person is obsessed with fear, he can recall 2 Timothy 1:7 and apply its truth to his situation. For example, as I was driving to campus to take my doctoral dissertation exams, I became overwhelmed with fear. I thought, "What if I fail the exams? What will I do?" At this point I quoted to myself that verse from Paul's letter: "God hath not given us the spirit of fear; but of power, and of love, and of a sound mind" (KJV). If I ever needed a sound mind it was then!

To my amazement and satisfaction, my fear disappeared and I went to the exams with a peaceful mind. That situation really made a believer out of me. God's Word can speak to the believer and strengthen him in ordinary human situations.

It is important to realize, however, that the Holy Spirit will never bring to your conscious mind any Scripture you have not memorized. Although it is possible to be impressed toward a specific Scripture and then look it up in the Bible and claim it,

God's Word can speak to us more clearly when we are familiar with it.

Another way the Scripture speaks God's Word to man is as "rhema." Has there ever been a time when you needed a word from God about a specific area of concern? Perhaps later you were reading the Scripture and suddenly a passage or verse leaped up off the page with an answer to your specific need. Later the truth of this word happened in your life. That's God's Word as rhema—the excitement of God working in the nitty-gritty!

One Labor Day weekend at a singles' conference at Glorieta, New Mexico, I was walking through the beautiful prayer gardens and a deep impression came into my mind to write a specific book. After my preliminary work had begun, the project bogged down. Almost a year later, on a weekend when I was speaking at a conference, a person came to me and told about a book she was working on. I was amazed that it was almost identical to my work. I did not know what to do. Because writing a book is such a difficult and time-consuming experience, I was determined to ask the Lord God for instruction concerning what I should do.

After approximately a month, one day as I was reading systematically in the Bible, a passage from Paul's writings did leap off the page and I knew it was the counsel for which I had asked (2 Corinthians 8:10–11).

> I want to suggest that you finish what you started to do a year ago, for you were not only the first to propose this idea, but the first to begin doing something about it. Having started the ball rolling so enthusiastically, you should carry this project through to completion just as gladly, giving whatever you can out of whatever you have. Let your enthusiastic idea at the start be equalled by your realistic action now. (TLB)

I said "yes" to God, got busy, and completed the work. A publisher was excited about getting the book. Wow! That's excitement: seeing God work in the nitty-gritty of life. You might laugh and try to explain God's work away, but I am a satisfied customer.

As a warning, however, remember that God does not always choose to work this way. As of today, I have only received a few rhema words in my life. On the other hand, the messages of God's Word as logos are available every day for the needs of the believer. In whatever fashion, let God speak to you through the Scripture daily.

Chapter Four
RESOLUTION

Assumptions for Understanding
the World

There are three different theoretical assumptions that describe how events happen in the world, as well as in human lives. These assumptions are important because they determine how an individual relates to and understands the world around him.

The model of *contingency* proposes that everything happens by chance. There is no form, order, or purpose in the world; events occur by accident, since everything is undetermined. Circumstances and occurrences cannot be explained, because there is no reason behind them.

Second, some people follow the assumption of *fatalism,* which holds that things are so ordered and structured no action or intention of any person can change events. The fatalist says, "Whatever will be, will be; there is no other way out of it." Several singles have adopted this pessimistic attitude because they can see no possibility or hope in their lives.

The third assumption, that of *certainty,* proposes the existence of absolute truth, which is real, unshakable, and unchangeable. There is a divine agent—namely, God—that works and directs events. The Christian who is living his faith accepts Jesus Christ as the way to God and the authority of the Word of God as truth. Therefore, the Christian should not try to resolve unpleasant events or problems by blaming God or circumstances.

Many people do not have the maturity to resolve bad events or negative aspects of their own character in an appropriate manner, much less to take the personal responsibility for actions and events. Some people blame God when something happens that is unpleasant, saying, "God could have kept this from happening if he would have. He did not, so I am angry."

After Bob and Cindy, two friends of mine, lost a child in a tragic accident, they responded by saying, "Why did God permit this to happen? He is all powerful; he could have kept the accident from happening. But he did not and we are angry! If God thinks he is going to get by with this, he has another thought coming!" Have you ever felt like blaming God?

Another way some people try to resolve bad events is to blame others. In the midst of a problem, the attitude is: "Someone else made me do it." The individual perhaps feels that another person acted wrongly and caused the problem; he believes that if others would behave correctly then he would be okay. An example is a student who complains about a hard teacher but never studies. He is therefore really to blame for his own failure.

Flip Wilson humorously expressed the desire to blame others by saying, "The devil made me do it!" Adam was more serious in the Garden of Eden. He blamed Eve for his temptations and problems. Eve blamed the devil for her behavior. Both Adam and Eve even blamed God at one point for their problems: Adam said, "Lord, the woman you gave me . . ." (Genesis 3:12 KJV).

Another scapegoat to blame is one's circumstances. It is easy for a person to believe that bad luck, improper timing, or circumstances beyond his control cause his problems. He feels that if a certain event had not happened, then he would not have gotten into difficulty. A person in this position usually takes the fatalist perspective, saying, "Poor me, I am just a victim of circumstances. Nothing I do is ever going to work out right. I am doomed to failure. Whatever will be, will be."

Some bad things happen because the person involved brings it upon himself. Sometimes, when an individual disobeys the will of God, sin is a part of the bad situation. The person in this case should be very careful to avoid visualizing God as an outlaw or cruel dictator. God might use circumstances to drive the wayward child back to him.

However, unpleasant occurrences are not always the result of sin. I always cringe a bit when someone says, "I know God did this to me to get even," rather than saying, "God can use this to bring about his will." Remember that not everything that happens is *of* God, although it can be used *by* him. This is the truth of Romans 8:28.

God cares more about you than you care about yourself! Resolve to look at circumstances—good or bad—as God-given opportunities for personal growth. Resolve to look at what God is doing instead of complaining about what God has not done.

Answer the following questions to become more aware of your theoretical assumptions for resolving difficulties in your life.

1. Give a personal example of how you think according to each theory for understanding the world.

A. I resolve difficulties according to contingency in these ways: _____

_____

_____

B. I resolve difficulties according to fatalism in the following manners: _____

_____

_____

C. I resolve difficulties through the certainty theory in these ways: _____

_____

_____

2. Give a recent illustration of how you resolved something by looking at what God was doing rather than what he was not doing: _____

_____

_____

Responses to the Activity
of God in Everyday Life

A Christian should *respond* rather than *react* to what God is doing in his life. This actually boils down to submitting to the sovereignty of God's work in life. The Christian must settle the question, "Is God in control of my life?"—and the answer will determine whether he reacts or responds.

A person often gets angry and reacts with an emotional explosion over anything that he feels is going wrong with his life. The basic root of reaction of this sort is usually insecurity and selfishness.

The response should be to get on with what God is initiating in one's life. Responding to God helps the individual get away from blindly doing anything to make something happen. Whatever the situation or circumstance, the Christian is to live above it, not under it! God wants his children to make use of all events to glorify him.

The manner in which the individual chooses to act determines the effect of events on his life. God can use even bad situations if the believer permits him the privilege. He can perfect, purify, and strengthen his child much as a metalworker passes steel through fire.

On the other hand, if the person reacts, it will only produce bitterness, hardness, defeat, and death. God's grace desires that events be used, but when human flesh reacts, it frustrates the work of grace!

When you have a frustrating, trying day, do you react or respond? Think of a day when you get up in the morning and are already tired. The reality moves in that your alarm did not work. You race to work, although every traffic light is red and cars are moving slowly, and you finally run into work late. Do you keep calm and trust the words of Paul concerning God's action in your life (Romans 8:28)? Do you choose to acknowledge God's sovereignty, give thanks, and endure? By responding you can find new insights into what God did for you to give you salvation.

First, *redemption* is the work of God *for* the Christian. Through God's holiness and perfect love, he made it possible for the individual to be removed from a position of death in Adam, and to be reborn into God's family through a position in Jesus Christ. In other words, redemption is deliverance from the bondage and consequences of sin because of what God did for man through Christ's atonement.

Second, *sanctification* is the work of God *in* the believer. To be sanctified is to be set apart for God's possession and use. For a person to dedicate, separate, and consecrate himself unto God is simply a response of faith to the separation—the sanctification—God works in man. Thus, sanctification is the work God did in man to set him apart for use in service.

Third, *service* is the work of God *through* the believer. God redeems, sets apart, and lives and serves through the Christian; service is "employment" of people by God to bring about his will and work in the world. In other words, service involves permitting God to use a life as a channel to affect other lives.

The letter to the Colossians reveals that believers possess the mind of Christ. In service initiated by God the mind of Christ shows in Christians and causes them to become fountainheads of evidence for the truth. God manifests what he wants to do in the world through his children!

God is working in the lives of Christians to get them to move from reacting to responding. A powerful verse concerning the scriptural way for a person to respond to God is 1 Thessalonians 5:18: "No matter what happens, always be thankful, for this is God's will for you who belong to Christ Jesus." (TLB)

Decision Making
and Discipline

It is difficult for most single adults to make major decisions in life, perhaps in part because so few have proper discipline in everyday activities. Scripture records many people who began with great success but failed at the end because they did not follow God's directions. Some of the most famous of these spiritual failures give us some insights.

God told King Saul to ban all witches, mediums, and wizards from the land during his reign. However, when Saul got desperate for knowledge, he instructed aides to try to find a medium to advise him. When Saul's kingdom fell, he was given the reason for his failure: "All this has come upon you because you did not obey the Lord's instructions." (1 Samuel 28:18). King Saul started with great success, but failed at the end because he did not discipline himself to follow God's directions. (TLB)

In the book of Acts, the story of Ananias and Sapphira is told. The two people sold some property and brought part of the money to give to the church leaders, claiming it was the full price. As a result of this lie, they fell dead. They began with an admirable goal, but failed at the end because of lack of discipline in telling the truth.

The Old Testament describes how Lot and his wife were directed to leave the city of Sodom. They were instructed not to look back as they left. "But Lot's wife looked back as she was following along behind him, and became a pillar of salt." (Genesis 19:26). What a price to pay! They started toward a new future, yet because of undisciplined actions, failure occurred. (TLB)

In your own life, there are probably areas in which you started out with great success, but failed at the end because of a lack of discipline. Success requires discipline! Discipline involves defining your goals, setting your priorities, and then fulfilling your commitment.

In order to lay the foundations for success, clearly define your goals. Think about your purpose in life; ask God, "Why did you make me and what do you want to accomplish in my life?" You will gradually learn, as you grow, what pleases the Lord God.

At specific times in life, I have become mentally immobilized and developed "analysis paralysis" as I determined my life goals. These experiences have produced four significantly personal priority perspectives and goals.

God is; I am; you are! Unless there is a dynamic interaction among the three perspectives of human and divine relation, the grand scheme of things is distorted. The first life goal for a person should be to be right with God, himself, and others.

In the second place, if a person fosters illusions (that is, treats things or concepts as true when they are not), he will become very disillusioned. The corresponding goal is to be realistically open to people and events as they are.

An individual is responsible for caring, sharing, relating, and loving, but he is not totally responsible for the responses of others. Goal number three is therefore to genuinely care for others but not allow unkind responses to offend one or make one feel inadequate.

The fourth goal is to be considerate, responsible, and productive in one's personal life, faith, and profession.

These four aims help illuminate where I place emphasis on success in life. My primary life goal is to live a life that is pleasing unto God.

As a person sets his goals, his priorities will become evident. Priorities, the plans that are written into one's schedule, help determine what is most important to fulfill goals. When a person does not have enough time to take care of some of the plans on his agenda for the day, then it is possible that part of the agenda was not initiated by God. A person has enough time to do what God wants him to do. Therefore, when time runs short, check to see if priorities are fouled up.

The Christian needs to practice the practical. A person practices daily what he believes; all the rest is just religious talk. Discipline of the body, mind, and emotions can possibly be learned by habit, but purposeful spiritual renewal and carefully nourished strength motivates a worthwhile and effective life.

Is discipline external or internal? Internal government is definitely preferable! For example, prayer and fasting have many purposes, but their major purpose is internal discipline and self-control. As a person denies his bodily appetite to eat food, he gains strength to rein in other bodily appetites and direct his energies to becoming mighty in spirit. When the Spirit is in control, an individual will have a greater understanding of discipline practicing the practical.

In order to facilitate practicing the practical, the process of decision making must be made clear. In the first place, decisions are not to be made on the level of feelings but on commitment. By an act of the will, a person commits in a decision to take a particular course of action. It is important to understand the relationship between decision making and the three aspects of faith: intellectual, emotional, and volitional.

Intellectual faith, which deals with the mind, involves the kind of faith-thinking that claims that God is, that he can do anything, and that he rewards those who diligently seek him. You probably hold to these basic tenets of faith-thinking. However, is God doing everything in and through your life that you think he can do? Thinking is only part of a real faith.

Faith is also emotional in that it involves feelings. Not only does a person *think* he wants God to work in his life; he *feels* an urgency for God to act in him. Faith as feeling causes the believer to wish, desire, want, and hope. However, feelings usually do not cause anything important to happen, and they do not bring about lasting commitments.

Faith as volition in its fullest power is willing commitment. Faith as an act of the will that leads to commitment is the formula that brings success in decision making. Every human being has a will—the ability to choose—which enables him to accept or reject alternatives and decide what must be done in any given situation. When the individual wills to act in a certain way, the body reacts to that will by carrying out its command.

The Christian must realize that action based on God's revealed truth is necessary in order for God to move in his life. To fulfill all the components of decision making the individual must mentally accept the facts and circumstances surrounding the decision; bring emotions into alignment; by an act of will, choose the best alternative for action; and then act! If a person only thinks he wants to act a certain way, he might later change his mind. If he feels he wants to act a certain way, those feelings might change later. Only by an act of the will can a lasting decision be made.

Learn to live by will rather than by emotions. For example, I hate running. Although I physically rebel, I know that it is good for me. I therefore make my thoughts and emotions submit to my will. The way I feel about running does not bring any benefit: only doing it counts. The only way for me to run consistently is to will to do it.

The issue is to build up the will to choose correctly. Although this is primarily a spiritual work, there are several things for which each individual is responsible in the process of decision making.

Get all the *facts* about all the alternatives. Leave no stones unturned. It is impossible for a person to make the right decision until he knows all of the possible choices.

Counsel with godly people. Without wise leadership a person is in trouble, but with godly counselors there is safety (Proverbs 11:14). It is usually not sufficient to talk to just one person. While plans go wrong with too few counselors, many godly counselors help to bring success (Proverbs 15:22). It is not wise to go ahead with your plans without the advice of godly people.

Be consistent with *Scripture.* It is the responsibility of the believer to read and know what the Word of God states concerning the many alternatives that he faces in the decision-making process. If something a person is considering doing is inconsistent with what the Scripture teaches, then he should not do it. He might pay a high price in one way or another for going against the guidelines that the Word of God sets. Study the passages of Scripture that relate to the particular situation.

Prayer and fasting are beneficial in opening oneself to receive

God's assistance. Trust God to give fruitful thoughts and impressions. God says, "Call unto me, and I will answer thee . . ." (Jeremiah 33:3 KJV). That help is what we really desire.

Prayer prepares the Christian to receive God's response and it changes his desire to conform to God's desire (Psalms 37:4–5). It also allows him to hear God's still small voice above the voices of counsel. That is important, because the believer must follow God rather than merely resorting to counsel from people. An example was when the apostle Paul was counseled against going to Jerusalem, to which he responded that God had called him to go (Acts 20:16, 22; 21:4, 10–14). If Paul's friends had succeeded in dissuading him from going to Jerusalem, he perhaps would have never made it to Rome.

Prayer also clears expectations of self and others. This makes the individual open to the responses of God even before they are given and provides the basis of God's revelation to him. Can you will to be willing to do what God wants you to do? If not, then you probably will never know his answer.

Prayer should be accompanied by fasting, either on an individual or group basis, when people are earnestly seeking directions from the Lord God. For example, Ezra 8:21 describes a fast called so the people would humble themselves before God in order to ask for guidance.

Waiting and living in the *presence of God* helps the believer to know the will of God. "They that wait upon the Lord shall renew their strength. They shall mount up with wings like eagles; they shall run and not be weary; they shall walk and not faint." (Isaiah 40:31). Isaiah records Israel's cry, "We wait for light" (Isaiah 59:9 KJV).

The Holy Spirit lives in the context of purity (Psalm 66:18). Is your life conditioned and purified for a word from the Lord? Purity is not too much a price to pay for answers!

Remember the last time you desperately cried out, "God, what do I do? Which way do I turn? What is right?" The answer is to be found in God's presence. I cannot tell you how, but you will know when you are in the presence of the Lord God. If you desire direction, seek his presence, because in his presence, he will reveal his way!

When Moses entered into the presence of God, the way was made plain. Regardless of how spiritually mature a person thinks he is, there will always be a Red Sea or Jericho Wall in his life. Each individual is constantly faced with decisions and the need to know the way from God. When a person does not know God's way, it is often an indication that he is not in the presence of God.

Commit to the best alternative revealed by God and put it into practice. After you have agreed with God concerning what he wants you to do, confess your desire and willingness to follow him. Bind the devil away (James 4:7–8) and praise the Lord God for the answer!

Decision making follows a logical step-by-step progression. When a person is guided by God, decisions are no longer such a difficult matter! A graphic representation of the decision-making process might be helpful to you.

The Decision-Making Process

Problem: state the decision that must be made
　　　　What matter requires a decision?

Data Bank: determine and gather available information from facts, counsel, Scripture, prayer, and the presence of God
　　　　What are the possible alternatives?

Possible Outcomes: logically explore each alternative
　　　　What is the final result of each possibility?

Desirable Outcome: evaluate data collected for each alternative
        in terms of importance
        What are the most important aspects of each possible
        alternative?

Point of Decision: summarize information and attempt to draw a
        conclusion
        Can a decision be made at this time?

YES	NO
Decision made	More information required
End	Return to Data Bank

The Joy of Commitment
and Involvement

Many singles are deeply lonely because they lack the joy of a
proper commitment to and involvement with self and others. At
a singles conference in Oklahoma City, Charlotte Weedman and
I were conversing about how many singles guarantee themselves
loneliness. Although the following methods to guarantee loneliness are presented humorously, there is a measure of truth in
them.

Stay away from the truth concerning one's feelings. Deny or run from
one's feelings. Do not face emotional responses. Blame someone
else. Do not find out what is causing one's feelings.

Stay away from the present, and live in the past or future. Continue
saying, "If I had not done that in the past, then . . ." "If only I
had . . ." Think about the future and say, "When I get . . ."
"Whenever . . ." Worry about oneself. Never involve oneself with
other people.

Stay away from prayer. Do not talk to God about problems, and do not be open to his responses. Above all, do not confess sins. Go ahead, be the captain of a sinking ship!

Stay away from the church. Be sure to not contaminate oneself by being around all those hypocrites! Do not let other Christians bear one's burdens or love one. For sure, do not go to church because there might be an opportunity to be a servant. One surely would not want to find meaning in helping someone!

Stay away from God. Do not act on faith; keep one's mind on temporal things. Stay anxious about everything. Do not try to relate to God because, after all, he is probably responsible for one's singleness.

In order to find a joy of commitment and involvement, the Christian must care, share, and relate to others. He must commit himself and get involved with God, others, and self. Many people use an acrostic to show how the joy of commitment in relationships is fulfilled when you place *J*esus first, *o*thers second, and *y*ourself third! Although this appears to be cliché, I urge you to go beyond the surface and dwell on this relational priority system.

From the greatest perspective, we only come into full being when we commit. Commitment is the basis of all relationships. Without it, there can be no communication that is a meaningful exchange or disclosure.

Tasting food is an analogy to commitment. When a person goes to a cafeteria, he might relate to the food with any of his physical senses. He might see, smell, and touch, but until he commits himself to taste, he will not know if the food is good. This is the way commitment works as well. Psalm 34:8 (KJV) says "O taste and see that the Lord is good."

Joy comes in risking commitments in relationships. "Nothing ventured, nothing gained," is a simplistic explanation of how risk plays a part in human relations. If you desire friends, then take the risk of being a friend (Proverbs 18:24a). Love takes risks! There are risks in telling the truth and being willing to submit to the responses of others.

Chapter Five
RENEWAL

The Need
for Renewal

The person who needs renewal finds himself in that position for one reason: he does not really have fellowship with Jesus anymore. The one who needs renewal is the one who has forgotten or lost a vital daily relationship with the Lord God in the areas of worshiping, praising, praying, depending, trusting, obeying, and loving.

In the New Testament Paul writes that the believer is to be transformed by the renewing of his mind. In other words, renewal comes when God's Spirit touches a person's spirit—not necessarily with a corresponding feeling that the Spirit is so doing. I have never seen any flashing lights in my head or heart as I read Scripture, but I know that God's Spirit bears witness to my spirit.

Manipulating God

Renewal is not what the needy believer is doing: it is what God is doing. Many times the Christian tries to manipulate God,

consciously or unconsciously, sometimes through deliberate
design setting out to force God to do things his own way. At other
times, the individual does not even realize that he is indirectly
doing God's work in his life.

The danger of trying to manipulate God is very real for the
Christian and perhaps is greatest when he most needs God. One
time that I was ill I went through all the stages of attempting to
have God work my way before I realized what I was doing.

When I first became ill, I thought, "This is no big deal. I will
just claim a Scripture verse from *the Word* for healing." So I
turned to the book of James, to the Scripture that concerns
healing (James 5:14–15) and demanded that God fulfill the
passage *my* way in *my* time. I said, "Lord, you say that if anyone is
sick, he should do the following things . . ." I did all of those
required things and I was still very ill.

I next thought that if I *prayed* hard enough and long enough,
God would have to give me what I was demanding. I called on all
my "prayer warriors" to intercede on my behalf for healing. It
was not long, however, until I realized that prayer was not
working—I was in fact becoming weaker. At this point, I decided
that healing perhaps had not come because of an improper
attitude on my part.

I then felt that if I truly *praised* the Lord for the illness, he would
have to change the situation and give me my demands. At first
only a half-hearted statement of praise came from my mouth.
After all, I was not going to lie to the Holy God by pretending that
I praised him for my sickness, because he knew my true attitude.

In a couple of days I worked up a sincere attitude of praise. I
was proud of myself, but my changed attitude did not work. My
physical problems were worse. I started trying to figure out what
else I could do to try to get God to heal my body.

Bargains, including attempts to play on God's sympathy, were
my next ploys. God did not respond to my new approach or bow
to my schemes. He knew me too well! He knew that I would say
or do anything to get relief from pain. From this, I realized

gradually that there was no way I could impress God or force him to do things my own way.

Disillusionment moved into my mind and my heart became discouraged. I asked myself, "Doesn't the Scripture work? Can't prayer change things? What's wrong with God?"

It was at this point that I realized that something was wrong with *me,* not with God. After several weeks of deep soul searching, I released my situation to the Lord God and asked him to reveal his purposes to me. There was nothing dramatic or emotional, but God began convicting me of several things. I realized that I had been trying to manipulate God through my use of Scripture, prayer, praise, and bargains. I wanted healing more than I wanted to know the Healer. I did not mean to short-circuit God's spiritual process; I just did not realize what I was doing.

Have you been trying to manipulate God? What do you have your spiritual eyes on now—the benefits of blessings or an intimate knowledge of the Blesser? If your attention is on the blessings, then you are robbing yourself of the joy of knowing the Blesser! When you reach the point at which you believe that the revealed Word of God is true regardless of what your senses or the circumstances around you tell you, you will live a life of victory.

Formula Is Not
the Answer

The true answer for producing renewal is not found in developing formulas, conducting meetings, or planning seminars. Many people are constantly seeking the formulas for miracles, successful meetings, fellowship, service, and relationships. The world of needy people is full of "miracle hoppers" and "meeting jumpers." These people usually are searching deeply but are often spiritually shallow.

When an individual realizes that he cannot manipulate God, he sometimes tries to make formulas for spiritual success. When one method works he tries to formulate that success to enable him to reproduce it. He then becomes superstitious, trying to do the same things to produce positive results. For example, if he used a certain phrase in a prayer and got positive results, then he will always use that same phrase to make something good happen again. After awhile, however, the glitter wears off his magic formula and good things stop happening.

Man-made formulas do not work; God does work. A person can neither second-guess God nor manipulate him through a formula that worked once in the past. The Lord God Almighty is bigger than plans, meetings, or formulas. Christians do need to plan and to meet together, and can sometimes even use formulas to help comprehend difficult points. But those that depend on only their own efforts to produce good events will probably be disappointed. It is the Spirit of God moving in a plan or meeting that makes all the difference.

Moving from the Milk to the Meat of the Word

As a person goes beyond formulas and attempts to manipulate God, he moves from the milk to the meat of the Word. The writer of Hebrews instructs Christians to refrain from going over the same old concepts and to move toward a mature faith (Hebrews 5:12–14; 6:1).

> You have been Christians a long time now, and you ought to be teaching others, but instead you have dropped back to the place where you need someone to teach you all over again the very first principles in God's Word. You are like babies who can drink only milk, not old enough for solid food. And when a person is still living on milk it shows he isn't very far along in the Christian life, and doesn't know much about the difference between right and wrong. He is still a baby-Christian! You will never be able to eat solid spiritual food and understand the deeper things of God's Word until you become better Christians and learn right from wrong by practicing doing right.
>
> Let us stop going over the same old ground again and again, always teaching those first lessons about Christ. Let us go on instead to other things and become mature in our understanding, as strong Christians ought to be. (TLB)

Paul describes his own spiritual journey in Philippians 3:12–14.

> I don't mean to say I am perfect. I haven't learned all I should even yet, but I keep working toward that day when I will finally be all that Christ saved me for and wants me to be.
>
> No, dear brothers, I am still not all I should be but I am bringing all my energies to bear on this one thing: Forgetting the past and looking forward to what lies ahead, I strain to reach the end of the race and receive the prize for which God is calling us up to heaven because of what Christ Jesus did for us. (TLB)

In describing his spiritual journey, Paul stated that he realized he had not learned everything; nor was he perfect. What a comfort those words are to Christians who consider Paul such a spiritual success that they see no hope for themselves in comparison to him.

Paul reveals that his life's aim is to become a truly mature Christian. The goal for every believer, therefore, should be to reach the level of "spiritual adulthood." To go from milk to meat seems difficult for most singles, who feel the world squeezing them into its mold. Yet people desiring spiritual growth have the same resources available to them today that Paul possessed.

There is quite a bit of talk today about the need for church renewal. It is a valid issue, and I do not know anyone who would disagree. The greater need, however, is for individual Christians to seek renewal. This will begin when individuals realize several key factors of the relationship between God and man.

The absolute seriousness of sin often blocks individual renewal. Proverbs 8:13 states that repentance from the *fruit* of sin is not enough; a person must repent of the *root* of sin. Some people love sin more than they fear God.

The absolute standard of God's holiness is a high requirement. Christians need an attitude of heart and mind that reflects life in the presence of the holy God. Isaiah recorded his experience of entering into the presence of the Lord God Almighty. He heard the seraphim singing to God: "Holy, holy, holy is the Lord of Hosts" (Isaiah 6:1–4). Holiness is the number one attribute of God. If a person really realizes God's absolute standard for holiness, he will "clean up his act!"

The absolute standard of obedience to God demands all of the believer. The usual concept of sacrifice is that it is most pleasing to God, but 1 Samuel 15:22 states that obedience to God is better than sacrifice. A "broken and contrite heart" is the sacrifice that God desires. Obedience is a ready response to God; rebellion is actually a response to false gods.

Perhaps the attitude is often "I want to be obedient, but I do not know how." The Holy Spirit will guide, direct, and teach the follower obedience to God. Also remember that delayed obedience is equivalent to disobedience!

If we, like Paul, press forward in Christ, we will grow toward spiritual maturity.

Moving from Sadness to Gladness

Most single adults must deal with sadness many times in their lives. At times, sadness seems to totally obscure any bright rays of gladness that might develop. One evening at Ridgecrest Conference Center a lady told me, "There is only one thing I hate worse than someone who is married, and that is a happy single!" Her honesty probably reflects the attitudes of many singles.

Some single adults enjoy being sad. One weekend at a conference in Mobile, Alabama, I met a very attractive lady. She appeared to be deeply sad, and gave no positive responses to any of my attempts to get to know her. When I asked the church's minister to singles about her problem, he laughed and said, "Oh, she enjoys being sad."

Some people think that being sad brings attention. It does! These people have not learned—or do not believe—that negative attention is worse than no attention at all.

There are some single adults who choose to be sad. Every singles' group has a "sad sack." I visited with a person of this type during a seminar in Springfield, Illinois. He said, "It's too much work to try to be positive, because nothing is going to turn out right anyway. It takes more personal energy to work on happiness." This response is a real cop out. People with this kind of attitude need to move from "doom and gloom" to "room to bloom!"

Moving from sadness to gladness is like spiritually moving from the picture presented in Romans 7 to the description in Romans 8. The person seeking gladness should ask himself, "Am I living in the *flesh* or in the *spirit*?" If he does not discover Paul's message in these two chapters, he will definitely end up in defeat.

Paul teaches that even after a person has had a salvation experience and is living a Spirit-filled life, he can still be defeated. He discusses the struggle that can occur within the believer (Romans 7:15–25a).

> I don't understand myself at all, for I really want to do what is right, but I can't. I do what I don't want to—what I hate. I know perfectly well that what I am doing is wrong, and my bad conscience proves that I agree with these laws I am breaking. But I can't help myself, because I'm no longer doing it. It is sin inside me that is stronger than I am that makes me do these evil things.
>
> I know I am rotten through and through so far as my old sinful nature is concerned. No matter which way I turn I can't make myself do right. I want to but I can't. When I want to do good, I don't; and when I try not to do wrong, I do it anyway. Now if I am doing what I don't want to, it is plain where the trouble is: sin still has me in its evil grasp.
>
> It seems to be a fact of life that when I want to do what is right, I inevitably do what is wrong. I love to do God's will so far as my new nature is concerned; but there is something else deep within me, in my lower nature, that is at war with my mind and wins the fight and makes me a slave to the sin that is still within me. In my mind I want to be God's willing servant but instead I find myself still enslaved to sin.
>
> So you see how it is: my new life tells me to do right, but the old nature that is still inside me loves to sin. Oh, what a terrible predicament I'm in!
>
> (TLB)

Can you identify with Paul? This man has the desire to do what God wants him to do, but he always comes up short! Remember that Paul, who really loved God, was at war with himself. Do you more strongly identify with poor Paul now?

The theme of Romans 7 centers on the concept of putting the old or flesh man to death. Paul gives some further instructions on this matter at another point in the New Testament (Colossians 3:5–8).

> Away then with sinful, earthly things; deaden the evil desires lurking within you; have nothing to do with sexual sin, impurity, lust and shameful desires; don't worship the good things of life, for that is idolatry. God's terrible anger is upon those who do such things. You used to do them when your life was still part of this world; but now is the time to cast off and throw away all these rotten garments of anger, hatred, cursing, and dirty language. (TLB)

A typical response is: "But I am not that type of a person!" Honestly, though, everyone has to wrestle with temptations of anger, impurity, malice, slander, and other sins. This is normal because humans have a sinful nature—that is, a tendency to yield to what Paul termed fleshly desire—and because Satan tries to make us disobey God's spiritual principles.

Another response might be: "But I do not practice those *gross* sins!" What about the advice Paul gave at another point (Titus 3:1–3)?

> Remind your people to obey the government and its officers, and always to be obedient and ready for any honest work. They must not speak evil of anyone, nor quarrel, but be gentle and truly courteous to all.
>
> Once we, too, were foolish and disobedient; we were misled by others and became slaves to many evil pleasures and wicked desires. Our lives were full of resentment and envy. We hated others and they hated us. (TLB)

How do human beings measure up to the Scripture now? Modern psychology is mistaken when it teaches that sinful attitudes must be expressed rather than curtailed and checked. One of my psychology professors once said, "The suppression of our feelings leads to the inhibiting and crushing of ourselves and our freedom." Scripture states that sinful feelings are not to be forced into the subconscious mind and ignored, but recognized for what they are—the individual's worst enemies. Those feelings should be confessed as wrong and put away.

When faced with a task of this magnitude, the believer often becomes discouraged and says, "It takes so much work. I grow weak in my struggling against the devil's temptations." The question is therefore desperately posed, "Who will free me from my slavery to this deadly lower nature?"

Paul gives some insights to answer this question (Romans 7:25b–8:4, 9).

> Thank God! It has been done by Jesus Christ our Lord. He has set me free.
>
> So there is now no condemnation awaiting those who belong to Christ Jesus. For the power of the life-giving Spirit—and this power is mine through Christ Jesus—has freed me from the vicious circle of sin and death. We aren't saved from sin's grasp by knowing the commandments of God, because we can't and don't keep them, but God put into effect a different plan to save us. He sent his own Son in a human body like ours—except ours are sinful—and destroyed sin's control over us by giving himself as a sacrifice for our sins. So now we can obey God's laws if we follow after the Holy Spirit and no longer obey the old evil nature within us. . . . You are controlled by your new nature if you have the Spirit of God living in you. (And remember that if anyone doesn't have the Spirit of Christ living in him, he is not a Christian at all.) (TLB)

Whereas the theme of Romans 7 is putting the old or flesh man to death, the theme in chapter 8 is putting on the new spirit man for life. As a person begins to try to put the old sinful nature to death, he becomes more dependent on the power of the Holy Spirit. To live in the spirit is for a person to trust the Holy Spirit to do in him what he cannot do himself. This is not a changed life, it is an exchanged life. It is Christ's own life that is reproduced by the power of the Holy Spirit in a person.

If I try to please God "in the flesh"—or under my own power and direction—then I am under the bondage of law. If I mind or pay attention to the things of the flesh, it brings death. If I mind the things of the Spirit, it brings life.

For example, as a young child, I was taught to mind my parents. When I did mind them everything was all right; it was life. But when I did not mind, things went from bad to worse. When my dad used the "board of education" on me for not minding it was not exactly death, but it was the next thing to it! This is what Paul teaches us in Romans: to mind the things of the flesh is death and to mind the things of the Spirit is life!

It is God who works in me. Weeping might endure for the

night, but joy comes in the morning of renewal when a person rediscovers God Almighty.

Rediscovering God Almighty

At a singles convention in Denver at which I spoke, the theme was "Rediscovering God." I concluded the keynote address with the statement, "I have come to realize that God is God and I am not!" The audience roared with laughter. During the entire weekend, I heard people laughing and repeating, "Well, after all, God is God and I am not." At the conclusion of the conference, the people had seriously realized the truth in that statement—a truth that is crucial if a person wants to remove barriers of self and come into contact with God.

How can a person rediscover God? In a way, I cannot say how an individual will know, but he will know when the Holy Spirit of God bears witness to him who God is and what the Christian life entails.

When a believer desires a renewed relationship with God, it is very helpful for him to examine the two prominent perspectives concerning salvation and the Christian life. One group claims, "When a person is saved he immediately enters into a completed relationship with God." The other group says, "After a person is saved, he must experience the filling of the Holy Spirit to complete his relationship with God." The first group stands strictly on the positional, judicial, historical truth of scriptural Christianity; the second group on experiential, personal, subjective truth. Rigid strictness makes both groups simultaneously right and wrong.

At the moment of salvation, the believer becomes judicially, historically, and positionally one with Jesus, receiving all that God has offered to him. However, perhaps due to a lack of knowledge concerning what the gift of salvation includes, the believer often discovers later what he possesses in Jesus. It is at that time that he becomes "experientially" filled—that is, that he becomes fully aware of the gift of salvation.

All truth is a balance, which when lost leads to error. Christians are often confused because many groups with conflicting ideas claim scriptural bases for what they believe and practice. Most of this confusion happens due to a misunderstanding of the terms the people involved are using. Keep this fact in mind: error and heresy are truth out of balance.

When I trusted Jesus Christ as Savior, I got everything I needed to serve him. My problem was that I did not know what it was that I got. My Christian journey since then has been a continual revelation of truths that are in no way new—they have been available for two thousand years.

The only time Jesus will work in my life is when he empowers me and gets all the glory. I am only a vessel or vehicle for God to live through. God is not necessarily interested in what my vessel looks like, as long as he can enter into me and live in me so that the world can see what he looks like through me. My Christian life does not involve God helping me, it is God living through me.

God wants the believer to cooperate completely and allow the Holy Spirit to illuminate and empower him. When a person rediscovers God Almighty, he will marvel at the power and peace of the renewed mind and spirit within himself. The Holy Spirit will take the Word of God and make it actual reality in the daily life of the individual. It will no longer be just a book to be read; it will become promises to be lived. When the Holy Spirit takes charge of a person's life, he will work in that life and turn tragedies into triumphs, shadows into sunshine, gloom into glory, and troubles into testing grounds.

Testing is very important for spiritual growth because it enables God to push a person into another dimension of spiritual meaning and determine if he will follow divine direction or strike out on his own. God will continue the test until the believer passes it, so the simplest course to take is to pass it the first time and save the painful trouble of a second exam on the same material. (The children of Israel took one test for forty years.) God will never take a person into another dimension of spiritual living until he tests that person's present spiritual condition. If he responds

correctly, God will supply him with new provisions and challenges. God will never forsake those who let his Word become
their rule of faith and practice.

I know that these spiritual principles are true, although I do
not always understand how they work. I do not understand
electricity either, but I am not going to sit in the dark until I learn
the fundamentals. I do not have to understand, I just have to
believe!

The major question is whether or not a person has given
himself to Jesus. If a believer does not meet the Father through
Jesus fresh in the morning, he will be stale by night. He must
make himself a gift to Jesus every day to enable Jesus to take him
and incorporate all he is into a divine partnership. In this way all
of the human life becomes God's; all of God's power and wisdom
become available to the believer.

God only takes and blesses what is available to him. The only
way for a person to live for God is to trust him so much that if he
does not come through, that person is through. God will never
move in an individual's life until that individual reaches the
position of looking only to God for answers. God will not
disappoint a person who has this kind of faith. This is the climax
of surrender to the Lord God Almighty!

It seems that God never moves in a person's life, whether it be
with regard to salvation or service, until he gets that person into a
time of desperation. Key periods of desperation come at "midnight" times in an individual's life, when figuratively speaking
there are hours of darkness to daylight either forward or back-
ward. It is at this point, stuck in the dark of midnight, that a
person cannot run out on God but must depend entirely upon
him.

As long as a person has tricks up his sleeve he will disobey God,
until he runs out of tricks. It seems that God ordained that
humans would reach a point of desperation, so that they would
abandon themselves to his power and glory! God permits a
person to have peace and power in his life as long as he acts God's
way.

One of the reasons God does not use some Christians for service is because they are not usable. For example, a rusty pair of pliers is not usable, but after they have been oiled and cleaned up, they are usable again. Sometimes Christians get rusty and have to be oiled by the forgiveness of God and cleaned up by confession (1 John 1:9) before they are usable.

The typical Christian talks big and walks little most of the time. As I was counseling with a single friend at a weekend conference in Dallas, she related that God was not using her as she desired. She finally concluded by saying, "Things are so bad that all I can do is trust God!" That conclusion should have been her first statement. When a person is cleaned up and trusts God for opportunity to be used, good things will happen.

Have you ever heard anyone repeat the maxim "God helps those who help themselves"? Although many people think it is a scriptural concept, it is not. When I hear someone say that statement, I always want to reply, "If you can help, then do it! If you cannot help, then shut up and let God do it!"

As God begins to move in your life, you will probably go through some form of spiritual warfare. Keep believing God even when you do not want to. Claim victory when the powers of hell come against you. Keep confessing what God has said about your situation even when it seems like he is not doing anything at that moment. In due time God will work!

Determine and practice scriptural principles. If God does not work according to your time schedule, relax and keep on practicing the principles. If God has promised something in his Word, it will work in the fullness of time. It does not matter if the principle is not working right now. Keep on trusting when you cannot smell, touch, taste, or see the completion of your hope. Hang in there! God will break through when he can get the most glory!

When a person is consumed by desperation and gets hungry for a demonstration of divine power, God will send a manifestation of himself and give that needy one a resurrection! People often try hard to push, trick, struggle, and manipulate with plans and programs. If they will get with God and obey what he reveals, he will move in their lives. There is nothing more meaningful than for a person to be where God wants him to be, and be willing to wait on God.

Do you know how to *wait* on the Lord God? One day in a restaurant I realized what it means to wait. As I was seated at my table, a waiter greeted me, took my order, and in a while served the food to me. At that point, I began to understand what it means to wait on God. I am to take his orders and serve him! Scripture gives explicit instructions for taking orders and serving God in this way. Meanings entailed by common usage of "to wait" are to look in expectation, to stay or remain ready for action, to take orders, or to serve. Let God reveal himself to you as you wait on him.

When an individual rediscovers the Lord God Almighty he will make his routine daily experience complementary with his position in Jesus Christ. As he waits on the Lord he will have

> Faith over feeling,
> Truth over tradition,
> Redemption over religion,
> New birth over baptism,
> Change over church membership,
> Deliverance over doctrine, and
> Fact over fear!

Chapter Six
RECONSTRUCTION

The Joy of
Being Motivated

Motivation refers to the process of including or modifying a response in a person by supplying attractive reasons for the desired behavior. Motives are any emotions or desires that operate on an individual's will and drive it to action.

Attempting to handle motives is like trying to pick up drops of quicksilver—they are elusive, irregular, and changing. Motives are extremely difficult to accurately determine in oneself or in others. Most people are often at a loss concerning understanding either motives or ways to get motivated. Most motives are deeply rooted in behavior that involves the satisfaction of needs.

There seems to be a common disease of acute laziness among many singles. They are not motivated to do anything and cannot explain why they feel so lackadaisical. The fact is, however, that single adults who are not motivated are usually down on themselves.

When I first started speaking at singles' conventions, it was evident that most single adults wanted to talk about how miserable they felt. They judged themselves as totally inferior to other people. As I walked across the grounds of Glorieta, I thought, "These people have come to have a pity party and celebrate their sorrow."

The quest to understand life continually causes some to raise the question, "Am I a complete and autonomous self or am I simply a projection of the wills and decisions of others?" Some people continue this poor attitude toward self by complaining, "Well, everyone else has everything so easy. Poor me. No one has it as difficult as I do."

When an individual does not have adequate fellowship with God and others, he usually is overtaken by this type of selfishness. The "poor me" attitude can cause his spiritual perception to become exceptionally dim and his physical nature to sink toward dominance by the world. Human beings were created for community and are incomplete without fellowships.

When a person is not motivated, he usually sits around and daydreams, gradually causing an unproductive mental fog. He feels at the mercy of any thought that races across his mind. Then consequent idleness lends itself to depression.

On the other hand, engaging in worthwhile endeavor builds self-assurance and an understanding of one's worth. The first step in doing anything is the desire to do it. Ask the Lord to put your "motivation gear" into motion. Make a realistic plan concerning what you want to do or to be. Oftentimes the doors of success or opportunity are marked "push." (Paul described this type of situation in Philippians 3:14.)

Analyze the process of motivation. Being an achiever sometimes requires discipline when no inspiration is around. Being disciplined in one's Christian life leads to motivation in other areas of life. Spiritual discipline produces physical, occupational, mental, emotional, and social determination to succeed.

The Christian should be the absolute best at what he does. The "best" does not mean the best among others in the world, but describes the highest point he as an individual can reach in relation to his potential (Colossians 3:23–24).

Work hard and cheerfully at all you do, just as though you were working for the Lord and not merely for your masters, remembering that it is the Lord Christ who is going to pay you, giving you your full portion of all he owns. He is the one you are really working for. (TLB)

Achieving Balance in Life

An individual needs to construct balance in his priorities. The discipline of the Christian life is found in the fact that the believer is dead to self and alive to Christ. The discipline of the one who has yielded himself to the Lord is the discipline of death to self, in which the person has no opinions except God's. Do not misunderstand: this does not mean that the believer who is dead to self no longer has any personality or self. It means that he is in cooperation with the Lord God to the extent that his motives and desires are in line with God's objectives.

The things that excite and "turn on" a person are the things that are really life to him. To the apostle Paul, Christ was life. Jesus excited him and made his life worth living. A valid test for evaluating the balance of our priorities is Paul's declaration: "For me to live is Christ, and to die is gain" (Philippians 1:21 KJV). Honestly fill in this blank for yourself, describing your balance of priorities. "For me to live is _____

_____

_____"

In giving this test to several singles' groups, many honest answers were shared. A young musician stated, "For me to live is fame and popularity, and to die is to be forgotten." A successful business person said, "For me to live is money, and to die is to leave it all behind." A student related, "For me to live is pleasure, and to die is emptiness." A young junior executive proclaimed, "For me to live is power, and to die is to lose it all."

If a person is going to keep his priorities in balance, then he must join Paul in proclaiming, "For me to live is Christ, and to die is gain." A person's day-to-day balance (or imbalance) of priorities communicates his real value system.

You are writing a gospel,
   a chapter a day,
By the deeds that you do
   and the words you say.

Men read what you write,
   Whether faithful or true:
Just what is the gospel
   according to you!

Sometimes an individual is getting nowhere so fast that he does not realize his imbalance of priorities. At times every Christian needs to slow down and examine himself.

Slow me down, Lord, I'm going too fast;
I can't see my brother when he's walking past.
I miss many good things day by day,
I don't know a blessing when it comes my way.
Slow me down, Lord, slow me down to a walk.

We must achieve a balance in our priorities.

Singles in the Church Family

A single adult needs to be a part of a caring, sharing, and supportive community of Christians. If he does not have access to a group of this type, then he can take the initiative to create one. However it is organized, the local church must constructively relate to singles. The church that understands the value of singleness and affirms those who are single, as well as those who are married, will have a great ministry of healing and wholeness!

The church can and should minister to singles in many ways. It can provide a place for single adults to meet and have healthy relationships and can form the basis for a caring, sharing, and supportive community. It can foster mutual interaction between singles and the church as a whole, as parts of the family of God. Some churches have a married congregation and a single congregation, and never the twain shall meet!

The church should take the responsibility of caring for the unique needs of formerly married persons. Widows, widowers, and divorced persons have been misunderstood and mistreated by people in the church, but the church needs to offer love and friendship to formerly married individuals, as well as to never married and presently married people.

The church should address the specific problems of singles. Included in this is a need to recognize and deal with the various levels of personal, social, academic, and scriptural development among the singles.

The church should realize and emphasize the scriptural fact that God is Father and that Christians are his children. In other words, God is our Father and we, the community of believers, are his family.

One time I asked my dad, "What pleases you?" He replied, "A happy family." As a family—brothers and sisters in Christ—we are to love and care for one another and promote happiness. Is your church characterized by a sense of family or is it a collectivity of strangers?

As people in the church see God as the Father, they will begin to function as a family. The Father loves, provides, protects, teaches, disciplines, comforts, and perhaps most of all spends time with the family. The family loves, forgives, sometimes fights, and tries to restore fellowship by making up.

There are biblical foundations for family support groups. In the Old Testament, God set up a covenant community based on divine requirements for life together (Exodus 20:12–17).

> "Honor your father and mother, that you may have a long, good life in the land the Lord your God will give you.
> "You must not murder.
> "You must not commit adultery.
> "You must not steal.
> "You must not lie.
> "You must not be envious of your neighbor's house, or want to sleep with his wife, or want to own his slaves, oxen, donkeys, or anything else he has." (TLB)

This covenant, designed for the welfare of each person's life and priorities, is also fundamental for family relationships.

When the basic principles are broken or discarded, the supportive community erodes. The prophets of God spoke loudly against such injustices in many passages of Scripture (Isaiah 59:1–8; Jeremiah 9:3–6; Hosea 12:7–9; and Micah 6:6–8 are examples).

The New Testament covenant instituted a supportive community of those who followed Jesus. "By this shall all men know that ye are my disciples, if ye have love one to another" (John 13:35 KJV). The followers cared for one another to a great depth of affection (1 John 3:14, 16 KJV). "We know that we have passed from death unto life, because we love the brethren. . . . Hereby perceive we the love of God, because He laid down his life for us: and we ought to lay down our lives for the brethren."

The kind of love that Christians should have one for another is described in 1 Corinthians 13. Although you have read this passage of Scripture many times, I encourage you to read it slowly and carefully with a view toward how Christians should love one another in a caring, sharing, and supportive community.

> If I had the gift of being able to speak in other languages without learning them, and could speak in every language there is in all heaven and earth, but didn't love others, I would only be making noise. If I had the gift of prophecy and knew all about what is going to happen in the future, knew everything about *everything,* but didn't love others, what good would it do? Even if I had the gift of faith so that I could speak to a mountain and make it move, I would still be worth nothing at all without love. If I gave everything I have to poor people, and if I were burned alive for preaching the Gospel but didn't love others, it would be of no value whatever.
>
> Love is very patient and kind, never jealous or envious, never boastful or proud, never haughty or selfish or rude. Love does not demand its own way. It is not irritable or touchy. It does not hold grudges and will hardly even notice when others do it wrong. It is never glad about injustice, but rejoices whenever truth wins out. If you love someone you will be loyal to him no matter what the cost. You will always believe in him, always expect the best of him, and always stand your ground in defending him.
>
> All the special gifts and powers from God will someday come to an

end, but love goes on forever. Someday prophecy, and speaking in unknown languages, and special knowledge—these gifts will disappear. Now we know so little, even with our special gifts, and the preaching of those most gifted is still so poor. But when we have been made perfect and complete, then the need for these inadequate special gifts will come to an end, and they will disappear.

It's like this: when I was a child I spoke and thought and reasoned as a child does. But when I became a man my thoughts grew far beyond those of my childhood, and now I have put away the childish things. In the same way, we can see and understand only a little about God now, as if we were peering at his reflection in a poor mirror; but someday we are going to see him in his completeness, face to face. Now all that I know is hazy and blurred, but then I will see everything clearly, just as clearly as God sees into my heart right now.

There are three things that remain—faith, hope, and love—and the greatest of these is love. (TLB)

Does the family of God love one another today in the way that this Scripture presents unconditional love?

At another point, Paul describes the "body of Christ" (1 Corinthians 12:12–14).

Our bodies have many parts, but the many parts make up only one body when they are all put together. So it is with the "body" of Christ. Each of us is a part of the one body of Christ. Some of us are Jews, some are Gentiles, some are slaves and some are free. But the Holy Spirit has fitted us all together into one body. We have been baptized into Christ's body by the one Spirit, and have all been given that same Holy Spirit.

Yes, the body has many parts, not just one part. (TLB)

Jesus described the church as his body and himself as the life of the body. While it seems that in many places today the life has gone out of the body, Christians in the early church were actively and intimately involved in the life of the body of Christ. Their witness to unbelievers and their deep love for one another caused the world to desire to know Jesus. How did they do this?

Some of the most obvious things they did were as a result of loving one another. They worshiped God together and prayed for one another (Philippians 1:3–4; 1 Corinthians 1:4; Acts 2:42). They also showed a desire to help and support each other, in conformance to the command "Bear ye one another's

burdens, and so fulfil the law of Christ" (Galatians 6:2 KJV). In order to bear burdens, an individual needs to share with others, to mutually open up and talk about the struggles he and they are facing. By sharing honestly, Christians involved in body support life can carry each other through difficult times.

Bearing One Another's Burdens[3]

In secular society and in many churches, people have been taught to play the game "Let's pretend." The rules are simply that the players pretend that they do not have any struggles or problems. Some think, "It is not spiritual to have problems. If I have problems, then I am obviously immature." Since no one wants to be thought of as spiritually immature, people sometimes cover up their problems and try to "look spiritual." That is hypocrisy! The first task in bearing burdens is to be open and to share honestly with one another.

The early church gave to the needs of others. It was a sharing group of people (Acts 2:41–47; 4:32–35; 2 Corinthians 8:1–24; 9:1–15). One's own needs are never so slight and easily forgotten as when one's eyes are focused on the needs of others. Self-centeredness and self-consciousness magnify one's own problems. The famous remark of William Booth always makes me stop and reevaluate my needs: "I complained because I had no shoes until I saw a man who had no feet."

A body is not just a collectivity of people put together. It is a living organism of which no part is dispensable. No one body part can carry out all required functions. The nose smells and breathes. Feet might smell at times, but their primary purposes are support and transportation. Each body part carries out its function and is specifically equipped for that task.

The church today, however, does not have this attitude of *unity,* but emphasizes the individuality of its parts. There are consequently few contemporary churches that have a scriptural body support life for their members to the extent that they should. For

Christians to promote the work of the church body, they must be as committed to the body as they are to the Lord God. For example, in the human body hands are as committed or bound to each other as they are to the head. If the hands could not get along together or work together they would not function properly, even if each got along with the head. It would simply not work. Every part of the body must be committed to every other part.

Next time you are eating the Lord's Supper, look around and ask yourself, "Am I as committed to being the brother or sister of each of these people as I am committed to Jesus as Savior and Lord?" When this degree of commitment comes, then body support life will begin to function in modern churches.

At a singles' convention in Houston, several people were talking about the role of the church in the lives of single adults. One man said that one of the roles of the church was to deal with "froghood." Everyone in the group instantly asked, "What?" Then he explained.

The "frog feeling" comes when a person thinks he is low, ugly, puffy, droopy, and pooped. He would like to be bright but feels dull; he wants to share, but is selfish. He wants to be thankful but is resentful; he wants to care, but is indifferent. Remember the old fairy tale?

Once upon a time there was a frog that was not really a frog. He was a prince who looked and felt like a frog since a spell had been cast upon him. Only a kiss from a beautiful maiden could free him. One day that happened, and he became a handsome prince again. You know the rest of the story—they lived happily ever after. So what is one of the purposes of the church? To spiritually "kiss frogs"!

Many churches across the nation are now constructing singles' centers as places for body support life to happen. These places give a Christian alternative to the promiscuous bar-oriented single lifestyle that predominates in secular society. The purpose of the singles' center is activities and spiritual enrichment for single adults.

Body Support Groups

Jesus stated, "I come that they might have life and have it abundantly." The point of the body support group is to help singles understand and experience more about what the abundant life in the body of Christ means. As the group understands the scriptural principles of group life, such impersonal concepts as theology and doctrine will be transformed gradually into exciting life-changing guidelines for functioning as parts of the body of Christ.

As in any other area of life, a support group must preserve balance, carefully avoiding extremes of thought or practice. A balance can be maintained in a group if the members make a covenant of friendship. In this covenant group members agree to treat one another as Scripture says that brothers and sisters are to relate—as friends.

The Bible states that a true friend always demonstrates affection and spiritual care. A man who has friends must show himself friendly; by acting friendly one can gain a friend who sticks closer than a brother (Proverbs 18:24). A true friend always shares with others what matters to him the most. A true friend always gives without limit even to the point of sacrifice. As people in a support group treat each other as friends, they will mutually give and receive.

Christians need to get away from clichés about body support life and make it happen! If your church does not have a singles' program, then do not wait for others in the church to come to you—you go to them. You might lose all of your spiritual energy or "rust" before anyone comes to you. In other words, it is a cop out for singles not to get involved with a local church because of a poorly developed singles' ministry.

I am a member of a small church in deep East Texas (where things have been done the same way for two hundred years) that does not have a singles' department or an established program. Since I chose to be a member of that church, I have two alternatives: I can be a "lone-ranger single," or I can become actively involved in caring, sharing, and relating with the members of the church. I have chosen the latter option.

Consequently, I did not wait for the church members to come to me; I went to them. I prayed that the Lord would show me how I could serve in this local church. I soon realized that in some ways we were hardly more than a collectivity of strangers who attended the same church, so I asked if anyone was interested in coming to my home to discuss our need for becoming a family of Christians. Many people responded favorably, and now we are involved in a body support group in addition to the regular activities of the church.

The group meets every Tuesday night at my home. Sometimes we eat the evening meal together and sometimes we have only an interaction time in which we get to know one another and relate our needs to each other. There are married people as well as singles in our group—anyone who desires to share and grow is welcome.

When we get together we have good times talking about recent events of personal importance to group members and entertaining each other. We also engage in some serious spiritual growth sessions. I usually prepare some questions, and we discuss our reactions and responses.

I have had no problems relating to this group as a single. A man said to me one night, "Are you not married? You act so normal!" His surprised response to singleness is a universal attitude in our society. But if singles act "normal" in a group environment, they can disprove many stereotypes. It is rewarding to see singles minister to one another and to married people inside and outside the church (1 Corinthians 3:21–23).

Many married people feel that singles do not want their fellowship; some think that singles prefer activities that include only singles. However, it is not necessarily true, and married people need to know that. Singles and married people can have meaningful times caring, sharing, relating, and loving in small body support groups.

The Church's
Ministry to Singles

Whether a church is large or small, it is possible to institute and develop a successful single adult ministry. Ken Gunter has developed a model of single adult ministry that outlines and discusses the four primary stages for building a singles' ministry.[4] By following these principles and the direction of the Spirit, church workers and interested members can labor together to build a new church work.

The first stage, *awareness,* requires that the church interested in starting a singles' ministry ask itself some fundamental questions: What does a single adult ministry involve? Why should this church start a new ministry? What has the church done for singles in the past, and what can it do now? What are the specific needs and problems of single adults that should be addressed by the new ministry?

Another factor in the first stage is to make the church as a whole aware of the discussion about the proposed new ministry. It is important that the entire church share in the ministry. If the church does not understand the need for a singles' ministry and does not support the early planning, then do not try it. Many churches have tried to begin single adult work when the members were not ready. New ministries often fail as a result in spite of a clear perception of the needs of singles, simply because the attitudes and feelings of the church body are not quite right. The church must support and share in any new ministry.

There are many methods to help a church become aware of singles and their needs. Plan a single awareness week, using creativity in special programs or fellowship meetings to help the church members to gain a better understanding of single adults. Sponsor community workshops and bring in outside people to speak on the issues that single adults uniquely face: single parenting, loneliness, adjusting to a couple-oriented society, and so on. Survey single adults in the church and the total church

membership for opinions, ideas, and questions about having a
single adult ministry.

A very wise move is to start the ministry with the support of two
or three key singles to insure success. Do not try to start without
church support. Do not foster the condescending approach of
ministry to "these poor single adults." There is no need to isolate
single adults from others; many do not like to advertise their
singleness. Single adults are church family members, too, and
they have needs and feelings like anyone else in the church. The
church should minister *with* them, not *to* them.

The second stage of development is *communication*—"How
should the church communicate with single adults?" Are they
really different from everyone else? No; the needs might be
somewhat different, but human beings are basically all the same.

Create an atmosphere for open and honest communication.
Encourage others to share how they feel and try to be really
concerned about their feelings. Help build relaxed and informal
relationships between singles and other church members. Do
not rush or force the communication flow.

This naturally leads to *leadership*. "What kind of leadership will
provide the best guidance for the ministry work?" In my experience the most successful plan for group direction is the shared
leadership approach, in which the interim or initial leader gradually severs the group from dependence on any one person and
encourages more and more group control. Under this plan the
leader exercises more control over the group in the beginning,
while at the same time encouraging more group independence
from his leadership.

By involving the group in the total process from the very early
developmental stages, the careful leader will allow the group to
take ownership. Almost imperceptibly, the group members will
take control of the group and will begin to exhibit a great deal of
pride in it. The leader ideally will then become an equal partner
in the group. He should remember to be flexible and sensitive to
this process, and not be quick to jump in and "rescue" the group
when it bogs down or runs into a problem. Let the members

work it out and struggle with it as a group.

This concept of leadership will be different from what many church leaders are accustomed to. Singles, however, have a need to be involved in the church as participants rather than just members. Each single can bring his unique gifts as given by God. The single adult leader should find the best place of service for each person, based on that person's gifts, and build the group together in ministry.

The leadership should also show qualities of *agape* love and forgiveness. A single adult leader should emphasize scriptural theology. He should realize that individuals are going to have a divergence of needs, and should strive to meet each single in the present situation.

The last stage for developing a singles' ministry is *organization*. Once a church has successfully completed each of the previous stages, it can begin to put the new ministry all together. "How should a new single adult ministry be organized?" The answer is a very simple formula: NEEDS + PEOPLE = PROGRAM.

Organization of a single adult ministry will be successful when the needs of single adults are discovered and steps are taken to meet those needs. Psychological theory reveals that a person's motivation is highly influenced by his own personal interests. Leaders cannot actually motivate people, they can only create a climate for motivation.

The formula NEEDS + PEOPLE = PROGRAM gets the needs of singles in the minds of the church members. Then the actions taken to meet those needs will be manifested in a motivated single adult program. Discovering, evaluating, and meeting needs are all part of the motivational process for developing a single adult ministry. As long as the formula NEEDS + PEOPLE = PROGRAM is used, and a continual process of discovering, evaluating, and meeting needs is carried out, the church will have a dynamic, motivated program. (Many churches experience failure when they use the "program to people" approach. This concept makes people fit into a program rather than designing a program to fit the people's needs.)

It is important not to get on the bandwagon of a single adult ministry until the orchestra is ready to play. The leaders should endeavor to discover the unique needs of their own single adults, match and analyze the needs discovered, and then develop the program.

Chapter Seven
RELEASE

Allowing Freedom

One of the basic dilemmas in life is centered around the question of how an individual can maintain his own personal freedom while at the same time obtaining the needed assistance of others toward reaching his personal goals. To the extent that he obtains the assistance of others, personal liberty is given up. To the extent that he preserves personal independence, assistance from others is lost.

Achieving individual independence usually involves negotiating with others to reduce their attempts to restrict one and to diminish their efforts to keep one dependent on them. Yet there has to be some interdependence because of the structure of society and because human beings must cooperate to solve mutual problems and often trade help or resources.

Individuals must mutually grant freedom to one another, and must enhance this freedom by creating a climate in which each person can be himself. Many times an individual does not feel free to be himself around others, because he feels that they are unfairly evaluating or judging him. A person must allow others the same freedoms he desires for himself. Many times individuals place unrealistic demands and expectations on themselves and others.

In order for relationships to be made free, a two-way release must take place. First, the individual must yield to others the right to be free. Although he will sometimes not give another the same freedoms he wants for himself, he must release that other to be his own self.

Second, the individual is free and can give himself the right to be free. If he does not please others, he still has the freedom to be himself.

Singles must free themselves and others in order to contribute constructively to others. Without the mutual exchange of freedom relationships will not be as healthy as they should.

The Joy of a Settled Mind

In the modern world people are desperately seeking peace and settled minds, trying to find release by many methods. Contemporary society offers "wine, women, and song," while God offers peace and a satisfied mind.

At one point in the movie *Jesus,* the people being taught by the Master heard him say, "Happy is the man who has no doubts as to who I am!" The answer to finding peace of mind is found in that profound statement. As a person comes to know who Jesus is, he is able to abide in Jesus (John 15:4). How can a person abide in Jesus?

Some help toward abiding in Jesus can be found in an acrostic using the word "abide." The word is broken up in this way:

*A*vailability. Believers must be available to relate to Jesus. I have learned that my availability is worth much more than my ability!

*B*iblical orientation. Christians must learn about Jesus through the Scripture. The Bible tells who Jesus is and how he wants us to relate to him.

*I*ntimacy with Jesus. To achieve peace Jesus' followers must be close to him. He will hold onto those who seek to abide in him.

*D*ependence upon Jesus. Christians must depend upon Jesus not only for life but also for power in living.

*E*xpectancy that Jesus will work. Believers must expect Jesus to do what he said he would in the Scripture.

As a person abides in Jesus, he understands more about the release and peace of God. God's every thought is for the happiness and personal peace of his children. "For I know the thoughts that I think toward you, saith the Lord, thoughts of peace, and not of evil, to give you an expected end" (Jeremiah 29:11 KJV). God does not want us to be frustrated or confused, for he "is not the author of confusion, but of peace" (1 Corinthians 14:33 KJV).

God's standard of success and peace is spiritual rather than physical. "For the kingdom of God is not meat and drink; but righteousness, and peace, and joy in the Holy Ghost" (Romans 14:17 KJV). God wants to give believers emotional tranquility: "The Lord will give strength unto his people; the Lord will bless his people with peace" (Psalm 29:11 KJV).

At a singles' convention in Albuquerque, I asked the listeners, "What are some of your greatest emotional difficulties?" The overwhelming majority of the responses included worry and anxiety. I was not surprised at this result, because everywhere I go, people are trying to find rest. Augustine proclaimed, "Lord God, you made us for yourself, and we cannot find rest until we find our rest in you."

Many single adults live with a painful uneasiness of mind. Worry and anxiety boil down to wrong and pointless thinking. Anxious worry is probably the greatest thief of joy, but the cure for worry is a peaceful mind (Philippians 4:6–7).

Don't worry about anything; instead, pray about everything; tell God

your needs and don't forget to thank him for his answers. If you do this
you will experience God's peace, which is far more wonderful than the
human mind can understand. His peace will keep your thoughts and
hearts quiet and at rest as you trust in Christ Jesus. (TLB)

In order to obtain the joy of a settled mind, the believer must
combat the worried mind through constructive thinking, praying, and living. The first goal, effective thinking, comes from
studying the Scripture. When I counsel a person, one of the
questions I always ask is, "What are you getting out of your Bible
study?" Most people respond, "Well, I really do not get anything
out of the Bible because I do not know how to study it." This is
sad, because believers need to realize the purpose of the Bible
and learn how to study it. The Bible is the Word of God, and it
shows people how to discover life that is eternal and authentic.
Bible study is meaningful to me because I have come to know
and love the Author. Through systematic study I get to know
more about God's love and plan for me.

There are several things to keep in mind while studying the
Scripture. It helps to know the setting of each of the books,
including who wrote the book, to whom it was written, and what
the circumstances were. Commentaries, concordances, atlases,
and Bible dictionaries are significant aids for understanding
God's Word. One of the most meaningful techniques of study is
to read the same passage from several translations or para-
phrases. Since the Bible is a spiritual textbook, the inspiration of
the Holy Spirit—the same Spirit who inspired the writers—must
inspire the reader as he studies. If this does not occur, he might
miss key truths in the passage he is reading. My basic stance
toward Bible study is therefore the attitude expressed by this
personal prayer:

> Lord God,
>   Just as holy men of God were inspired by the Holy Spirit to
> write this Scripture, so also I trust the Spirit to illuminate my
> heart and mind as I read the Bible, that I might know what you
> want me to know and do!

It works! I am a satisfied customer! I encourage you to adopt this basic view toward your Bible study. Let God speak to you today in your present condition and circumstances; he understands you and your world.

Inspired and careful Bible study will teach the Christian how to think effectively. Paul profoundly advised, "Fix your thoughts on what is true and good and right. Think about things that are pure and lovely, and dwell on the fine, good things in others. Think about all you can praise God for and be glad about" (Philippians 4:8). Every thought must be brought to Christ in obedience. (TLB)

> Sow a thought, reap an action
> Sow an action, reap a habit.
> Sow a habit, reap a character.
> Sow a character, reap a destiny!

The second way to combat a worried mind is to pray effectively. Prayer is conversation with the Lord God, and it is vital to the growth and spiritual health of the believer. One way to help keep in mind the four component parts of prayer is the acrostic "acts."

A doration. Adore God for who he is! He is Father—the Creator; Son—the Savior; and Spirit—Comforter and Illuminator. He calls to us, saying, "Be still, and know that I am God!" (Psalm 46:10 KJV). The believer should empty his mind concerning himself and think about who God is!

C onfession. Confess sins to God. "If we confess our sins, he is faithful and just to forgive us our sins, and to cleanse from all unrighteousness" (1 John 1:9 KJV). Confession is not simply a remorseful feeling about botching something. It includes the definite act of repentance—turning around—and the gift of God's forgiveness.

T hanksgiving. Thank God for who he is and what he is doing. "In everything give thanks: for this is the will of God in Christ

Jesus concerning you" (1 Thessalonians 5:18 KJV). A spirit of thanksgiving will carry over into one's thoughts and actions.

*S*upplication. Make requests to God for your own needs and for the needs of others. God has promised to guide his children in every aspect of life. "Trust in the Lord with all thine heart; and lean not unto thine own understanding. In all thy ways acknowledge him, and he shall direct thy paths" (Proverbs 3:5–6 KJV).

Paul instructed Christians to be in constant communication with the Lord. Believers should also discipline themselves to schedule definite prayer times each day. And regardless of how many other people an individual prays with during a day, he must have some personal and private prayer time.

Find a place where you will be free from interruptions to pray. As you communicate with the Lord, keep in mind that there is no one around to impress. Tell it the way both you and God know that it is! God always does business with those who tell the truth.

Another acrostic, made with the word "prayer," points out important attitudes that the believer should cultivate in prayer.

> *P*eruse the nature of God
> *R*eexamine self
> *A*ffirm the Scripture
> *Y*ield self to God
> *E*xpect God to work
> *R*ejoice!

A third method of combating a worried mind is to live effectively. Inward attitudes and outward actions both give evidence of the quality of life an individual is living.

Living according to the direction of Scripture is a necessary condition for experiencing the peace of God. It is one thing to merely learn a scriptural truth; it is quite different to incorporate that truth into one's life, putting it to work in thought and action.

Paul challenges believers, "Be ye doers of the word, and not hearers only" (James 1:22 KJV).

The presence or absence of the peace of God is a good test for a Christian to see if he is living according to the will of God. If a person is walking with God, he will have the peace of God in his heart. When he disobeys God, he loses that peace and becomes aware of the fact that everything is not right. "Let the peace of God rule in your hearts" is the command given in Colossians 3:15 (KJV).

It is easy to understand that effective praying, effective thinking, and effective living are the conditions for having a secure mind and victory over worry and anxiety.

Letting God
Be God

It is frequently difficult for people to avoid attempting to play the role of God. Because human beings cannot know everything about God, they often are tempted to explain God's nature or plan in their own terms. By doing this they often presume a complete knowledge of God. I have learned not to use absolute terminology anymore when talking about God's ways. He docs what he wants in his way and in his time! (Simply speaking, "God is God and I am not.")

For a person to have a good relationship with God, he must yield to God the right to direct actions and attitudes. If this stance is not taken, God will probably not provide any direction at all. The choice is to do things God's way or risk that they will not be done right. God wants the believer to trust him alone! We have to be willing to be vulnerable and honest with God.

In order to "let God be God," the follower must recognize and trust divine sovereignty. The notion of God's sovereignty is the supreme principle of Scripture. One man concluded a discussion with me about God's sovereignty by saying, "If God is not sovereign, then I am a wretched, disillusioned man indeed! But time keeps proving that he is completely sovereign!"

Trusting God's sovereignty entails believing that he is available to help his children. Scripture reveals the many ways that God is available to assist and guide those who trust him.

The Bible first makes clear that God is in the position to meet the needs of human beings. As the Almighty, God has the power to create, sustain, and rule the universe and mankind (Romans 1:19). God is still in a position to meet man's needs even though the Fall has obstructed free contact between man and God. God is therefore available to believers because he is in the position to assist them.

Second, God is available to Christians on a conscious or mental level. Scripture proclaims: "The Spirit itself beareth witness with our spirit, that we are the children of God" (Romans 8:16 KJV). In other words, the ability to know God is within the mind or heart of every person. How wonderful it is to know that the Lord God Almighty, who has the power to create, rule, and sustain the universe, has made himself available to be known by his creatures! When God's Spirit makes him known to the inner conscience of a person, that person can have peace with God by trusting Jesus as Savior and relying on the power of the Holy Spirit. As a result, peace with others will then follow.

The third way that God is available to his children is through the Holy Spirit's manifestations of his character. "The love of God is shed abroad in our hearts by the Holy Spirit which is given to us" (Romans 5:5b KJV). In other words, the Holy Spirit manifests God's nature within followers of Jesus Christ. "The fruit of the Spirit is love, joy, peace, longsuffering, gentleness, goodness, faith, meekness, temperance" (Galatians 5:22–23a KJV).

God is therefore available for help and able to work in the lives of believers. This is possible because he is in the position to do so and has the power to act, because he created humans with the potential to know him, and because he has given the Spirit to recreate godly characteristics in human lives. As Christians yield and "let God be God," they will move from the wilderness of human endeavor to the promised land of divine sovereignty. The termination of self-controlled life and the beginning of life in Christ occurs when that Jordan River is crossed.

The Christian life is both objective and subjective. The objective truth of the revealed Word of God must be known and obeyed; the subjective experience of God working in life is to be enjoyed. However, experience must always be subject to Scripture.

The Lordship of Christ

An important correlate to "letting God be God" is for the believer to proclaim Jesus as Lord of life. Many single adults are not experiencing any joy of salvation, and consequently many have given up in defeat. It is obvious to me at conferences and seminars that many singles are brokenhearted, yet they often refuse to commit the lordship of their lives—that is, the right to direct their lives—to Christ. This occurs because they are afraid to step out in faith.

There is an important difference between Jesus Christ's roles as Savior and as Lord: Jesus the Savior is received by the believer; Christ the Lord gains control of the believer. Christ will assume lordship of a believer's life only as a result of a vital two-way relationship.

The concept of lordship is difficult to completely define. I think that Christians have missed the full meaning of lordship by looking for a stuffy, theological explanation of what is actually a vital and living relationship. Simply expressed, lordship means that Jesus Christ is the boss and that he makes the decisions. When a Christian spiritually "sells out" lock, stock, and barrel, Jesus becomes the sole owner. He therefore does not ride in the back seat; he drives!

Lordship sets the Christian life in motion and causes the believer to be productive, peaceful, and joyful. This process yields a positive attitude and releases the tension of life. When a believer accepts God's will for him and yields the lordship of his life to Christ, it produces excitement in his life.

It seems that ignorance and rejection are the major reasons

Christians have missed the benefits of having Christ as Lord. Some singles fail to accept the life of faith because it is not necessarily easy. Lordship is more than a doctrine to be believed and declared—it is a relationship to be lived!

Has there ever been a period in your life when all that you were and had at the time was subjected to the Lord? Have you reached the point of giving in to him? "God, I am finished with trying to run my life. There is not one thing in me that I have done that is worth redeeming. I yield to you; I declare myself dead and you alive in me!"

For a long time I copped out and avoided yielding to Christ by trying to formulate lordship and reproduce the experiences of others. I read all of the classic works concerning Christ's lordship and listened to countless numbers of speakers. I then decided to try to make a lordship commitment. I tried to yield control of my life to Christ the way Jack Taylor says, but nothing happened. I reread Watchman Nee and tried his principles; that did not work either. I tried to combine the best of what I had read and heard in the past about Christ's lordship, but nothing worked.

One afternoon, as I walked in the forest near my neighborhood, I began talking desperately to God about Christ's lordship and my life. I said, "God, I have tried to follow the ideas of all of the spiritual giants concerning making Christ Lord, but nothing seems to make any difference. I suppose I do not care what all those other people have done; I am here to do business with you on your terms for me. By faith I accepted Christ as my Savior. Now by faith I release myself and the lordship of my life to him. I want to praise him for being my Savior and Lord."

As I completed my prayer, I found a new sense of closeness to God Almighty. I just praised the Lord—in ordinary English words—and I found the peace that accompanies Christ's lordship. Consequently, my advice is that you not try to reproduce the experience or formula of Watchman Nee, Jack Taylor, Jim Towns, or anyone else; do business with the Lord in your life on his terms. God is best able to work in those who are honest with him.

When a person commits the lordship of his life to Christ, he gradually learns to worship the Lord rather than the gifts and blessings that are given to him. Christ's lordship requires that his subject be obedient and reverent and have right motives. Nevertheless, whatever God requires of a person, he will also perform through that person. When the Holy Spirit makes a believer aware that he needs the lordship of Christ in his life, God is also saying, "I am ready to provide that leadership, if you will *trust* me."

One day, "at the name of Jesus every knee shall bow in heaven and on earth and under the earth, and every tongue shall confess that Jesus Christ is Lord, to the glory of God the Father" (Philippians 2:10–11). Everyone will eventually confess that Jesus Christ is Lord—some the hard way, others easily.

When I was a child, I hated to go to bed at night. One night when my parents told me it was time to go to bed, I hesitated, trying to think of a way to stay up later. My Dad said, "You can go easy or hard, but you are going to bed. The choice of how is yours."

I believe the Holy Spirit communicates to every person Jesus' question: "Will you make me Lord of your life? You can come the easy way or the hard way, but you are going to come. The choice is yours."

A Living Personal Faith

In order for an individual to "let God be God" in his life, he must appropriate the Scripture and incorporate it into his experiences. The believer needs to quit admiring how God is working in the lives of other people and start applying the Scripture to his own life. In this way a life under the lordship of Christ will gradually be built into a life of outstanding faith.

First, the believer must realize that everything he needs spiritually and physically has been appropriated for him by God. All blessings are his in Christ: "Blessed be the God and Father of our Lord Jesus Christ, who hath blessed us with all spiritual blessings in heavenly places in Christ" (Ephesians 1:3 KJV).

God has not only appropriated the fulfillment of the believer's required needs, but will give him sufficient increase as well. "God is able to make all grace abound toward you; that ye, always having all sufficiency in all things, may abound to every good work" (2 Corinthians 9:8 KJV). God's appropriation includes health in addition to spiritual and life needs. "Beloved, I wish above all things that thou mayest prosper and be in health, even as thy soul prospereth" (3 John 2 KJV).

Second, the Christian must accept what God has appropriated or made available for him. The believer enters into salvation by faith, but often does not continue the life of faith. Faith is not only the door to salvation, it involves taking steps, confessing the Word, making decisions, and—sometimes—waiting for answers.

Many singles trust God to take care of eternity but do not entrust the present to him; many do not believe he will supply their daily needs. If a person has turned over his eternal life to God, is it unreasonable for him also to trust God with daily needs? God is concerned with life *now!* Move from complaining to claiming. Until a believer gets to the point that he believes the Scripture is true regardless of what his thoughts or feelings tell him, he cannot live a life of victory. "We walk by faith, not by sight" (2 Corinthians 5:7 KJV). Most people have faith, but lack the everyday experience of believing what God will do in the present—that is, a *living* faith.

Faith can be viewed from two perspectives. The first, which deals with the facts, doctrines, or concepts that the Christian believes, concerns the *content* of faith. On the other hand, the way that the Christian entrusts himself to God's care and relies on his relationship with God to sustain him is the *act* of faith. Both aspects of faith must be exercised in order to please God. The believer's attention to the content of faith saves and keeps him; the act of faith releases God into everyday life so he can show himself great, bring honor to his name, and edify his children (2 Chronicles 16:9).

Do you have active faith? For what are you trusting God *now?* What has he told you to trust only him to give, so that he might show himself strong in your behalf in a vivid and real way?

Living faith is the process by which a person finds what God would have him do in his present situation, and then takes action. That is the true point of faith. Will you do what God has instructed you to do, and trust him for the results even when those results are not visible as yet? Active faith is not measured in terms of quantity or quality, only in terms of obedience. Faith is not blind or reckless behavior; it is finding out what action God desires and then being obedient. Obedience releases God to bring the result to pass.

Remember that no sin displeases God more than disbelief (Revelation 21:8). When Jesus returned to his home town, he did not work miracles there simply because of the unbelief of the people (Matthew 13:53–58). God has chosen to relate to human beings only by faith. Despite this fact, all Christians doubt at one time or another. The famous faith chapter, Hebrews 11, tells about the many exciting events that happened because of faith. It also warns about the consequences of unbelief. (I am often like the epileptic's father in Mark 9:24 [KJV]: "Lord, I believe; help thou mine unbelief.")

When the believer truly comes to know the appropriation that God has planned to supply his needs, and accepts or claims that appropriation by trusting God's Word, he will enter into the rest that living faith gives. Do not misunderstand: there might be a waiting period between claiming and receiving God's gifts. (For example, Abraham and Sarah had to wait twenty-four years for Isaac. After ten years, they began to disbelieve God and tried to produce a child their own way. Despite the chaos they caused, God came through in his own time.) The believer will be kept waiting until he knows that his needs are supplied with gifts from God alone. Then he will glorify the Lord God.

Therefore, faith is discovering the will of God revealed in his Word and believing, claiming, confessing, and acting upon that will. Since faith is based on the revelation of the Scripture, it is therefore not "blind" or presumptuous. The believer can only trust God for what he has been instructed by God to do. "Faith cometh by hearing, and hearing by the word of God" (Romans 10:17 KJV). In order to "let God be God," the Christian must have faith!

Chapter Eight
REJOICE

Discovering
Personhood

The advertising industry has created an illusory "joy." Television commercials promise the "good life" if listeners buy certain brands of products. Many people probably become disillusioned when they buy the "right" brand and it does not bring the promised results. They then often blame or doubt themselves for their lack of joy. The truth is that Madison Avenue versions of joy are not really joyful.

Every person has a deep desire to feel adequate and joyful in all circumstances. However, most people know how to *appear* to be happy and well adjusted regardless of how lonely or hopeless they truly are. The problem with good appearances is that they do not satisfy deep personal needs.

When the Christian single discovers his personhood, place, profession, and promise, he knows the true joy inspired by the Lord God. When he really discovers who he is, then he is able to rejoice as a fully functioning self, an individual that is fulfilling his potential and relating properly to God and others.

The fully functioning Christian first accepts and holds to

119

Christian values and beliefs. In other words, he completely accepts Jesus Christ as Savior and Lord of his life. This person has more than an intellectual knowledge of Jesus—he comes to know the Lord through revelation. He determines his life's values and priorities on the basis of his Christian commitment.

Second, the fully functioning Christian single lives life only in the spirit of the Christian faith. This person has no need to deceive others or shift behavior continuously, depending on the people nearest him. Because he is motivated by faith in God, he does not constantly have to analyze his past behavior to appear to be consistent in the present.

Third, the Christian single sees his status as a combination of being and becoming. "Therefore if any man be in Christ, he is a new creature: old things are passed away; behold, all things are become new" (2 Corinthians 5:17 KJV). I describe my own nature of being and becoming in this manner: "I am not what I ought to be; I am not yet what I am going to be. But thank God, I am not what I used to be!"

Fourth, the fully functioning Christian thinks well of himself and others, recognizing the value and dignity of every person. Every person has significance because Jesus died for him; God loves every individual! That makes human beings significant and important (Romans 5:8). To think well of self and others opens up a whole world of possible relationships.

Fifth, the fully functioning self sees value in the mistakes he and others make, and attempts to correct those mistakes. He knows that he will encounter new circumstances and problems all the time, and he recognizes that he will not always render correct judgments and responses. He realizes that mistakes are inevitable when constantly "breaking new ground," but will utilize unprofitable paths to show the way to better ones. The person makes the worst mistake who never learns from his past mistakes.

One step toward discovering one's personhood is to become employed in a fulfilling vocation. The Christian should rejoice in the work to which God has called him (Colossians 3:23-25)!

Work hard and cheerfully at all you do, just as though you were working for the Lord . . . , remembering that it is the Lord Christ who is going to pay you, giving you your full portion of all he owns. He is the one you are really working for. And if you don't do your best for him, he will pay you in a way that you won't like—for he has no special favorites who get away with shirking. (TLB)

Vocations and jobs are means to an end—for the Christian that end is to glorify God. The danger is that a job will become an end in itself. We do not think of Paul primarily as a tentmaker, nor Luke as a physician, nor Matthew as a tax collector, nor Peter as a fisherman. This is the case because each of these men regarded his faith as his true vocation. Christians should walk by faith in the same way and take care not to misplace the importance of security on a job, but put full trust in the person Jesus. When an income-producing job does not enable a Christian to fulfill his life's vocation of faith in Jesus, he must seek employment elsewhere.

The True Source of Joy

God is the sole source of joy; other men or lucky circumstances are not. Many people think of joy as a memory of some event in the past or a longing toward some fulfillment in the future. On this view, joy is an occasional blessing rather than a regular experience. This perhaps explains why many seek pleasure as a temporary escape instead of aiming for a constant and fulfilling joy.

Joy is not a commodity for sale. Joy is not often found in the absence of pain; it usually becomes one's possession as one learns to live with sufferings. It slips into the soul of the believer who is serious about proclaiming Jesus Christ as Savior and Lord of life. The gigantic secret of the Christian is joy, which comes into the faith-directed life in the same way that peace does. After the believer has made certain decisions about goals and priorities and begins to put them into practice, then joy unobtrusively enters his life.

Joy is a spiritual quality of life that transcends happiness and pleasure and makes those who possess it companionable and radiant. In other words, joy is the delight of true fulfillment. The source of joy is a purpose much greater than self—the completion of God's plan.

Good humor is one of the principal characteristics of joy. Christians need a healthy sense of humor. Sometimes believers get so serious and so heavenly minded—so wrapped up in religion—that they serve no useful purpose on earth. I am confident that Jesus and the disciples had a happy good time laughing about many of the events that happened during their travels. It is okay to relax, to laugh, and to celebrate life!

Joy can be obtained by any person who is willing to receive it, but it is not going to be delivered on a silver platter. It will commence as the believer commits himself to be open to experiencing it and open to God's direction. I do not mean that Christians should go out on "treasure hunts for joy." Simply follow the lordship of Christ and free self to experience joy. One single I know says, "We are about as happy and joyful as we make up our minds to be."

> A bell is not a bell until you ring it,
> A song is not a song until you sing it,
> A joy is not a joy until you share it.

Joy is not the same as happiness. While happiness depends upon circumstances, joy is based on dependence upon Jesus regardless of circumstances. Happiness usually depends on good happenings, but even when things go wrong a person can have joy if he so chooses. I encourage Christians to be joyful, because it sure beats just being happy!

If a person requires good events to feel happy, then he does not possess the joy that God gives. When God is the source, joy remains steady despite the ups and downs of life. Joy is the most infallible sign of the presence of Jesus in a person's life.

Christians must beware of several matters that, unless controlled, will rob them of their joy. Perhaps the most obvious thief of joy is *circumstances*. Most people would admit that when things are "going their way" they are very happy and are very easy to get along with. When times are tough, though, some are more comfortable with becoming martyrs—rolling over and playing dead—than they are reexamining their circumstances and acting to change whatever they can. Happiness and unhappiness are ultimately derived from the way circumstances are perceived and evaluated; the person with a joyful disposition always views circumstances positively.

No one has ever escaped losing joy because of the unkind remarks or deeds of *other people*. The problem with this thief of joy is a basic lack of honesty with self. People are always accusing or blaming someone else; it seems so much easier to pass the buck. The answer to this is the powerful truth that the only person who can keep a person from having joy is *self*.

Things or *material possessions* can be great thieves of joy. If an individual seems to lose his joy when there is a problem with his material possessions, he should ask himself this question: "Do I own these things or do they own me?" Jesus said that "a man's life consisteth not in the abundance of things which he possesseth" (Luke 12:15b KJV). One day Jesus taught his followers, "Lay not up for yourselves treasures upon earth, where moth and rust doth corrupt, and where thieves break through and steal: but lay up for yourselves treasures in heaven, where neither moth nor rust doth corrupt, and where thieves do not break through nor steal: for where your treasure is, there will your heart be also" (Matthew 6:19–21 KJV). A great number of people think and act like joy comes from the things they own. In reality, it is possible for the love of possessions to rob people of the only kind of joy that will really last.

The worst thief of joy is probably *worry*. Worry is doubly negative, because it has not only mental but physical consequences. Medicine might remove the symptoms of a worried mind, but it cannot remove the causes. In other words, a person can purchase "sleep" at a pharmacy, but he cannot purchase "rest" anywhere. God alone has a spiritual prescription for worry (Philippians 4).

The Joy of
Continued Growth

Joy comes to the person in the process of becoming when he realizes and makes use of the significant truths he has learned. I believe that Christian single adults continually receive new insights in their pilgrimages through life. There are several things to keep in mind in the daily expression of the joyful life.

Keep in mind that Scripture is the gauge for analyzing truth, not experiences. The Word of God has more authority than any experience I have ever encountered. Experiences concern subjectively based emotional responses or evaluations. These responses and evaluations give rise to feelings, which cannot always be trusted.

Scripture sets up explicit gauges for measuring events that are encountered in life. Experience should be evaluated in light of Scripture rather than Scripture in light of experience. Scripture is the objective truth of God; experience is at best the subjective interpretation of Scripture.

Life is a flowing, changing, relative process. I find that life is richest and most rewarding when it is flowing toward a goal determined by the unchanging truth of the Scripture. This is both fascinating and a little frightening. I find that I am at my best when I flow in a direction toward goals of God's will for my life. In this complex stream of my experience, I try to understand that the only fixed point or absolute is the Word of God.

The person who is growing in joy must accept and understand self and others. It is very important for the Christian to come to understand and accept himself as being what he is solely by the grace of God. It therefore becomes easier to accept oneself as an imperfect person of the type described by Paul in Romans 7, who is striving for—yet not always reaching—the goals outlined in Romans 8.

To truly accept another person and his feelings is by no means an easy task. Some modern psychologists propose that acceptance of others requires that every person feel and think in the same fashion. Contrary to this claim, however, people must sometimes agree that they disagree, or disagree agreeably. There are also times when the Christian must tolerate other views but not compromise his own values or beliefs.

The joyful person must share with others and let others share with him. Scripture continually reveals that the believer is to care for others and let others care for him in a two-way relationship. The prayer of St. Francis provides an excellent expression for the ideal lifestyle of every single adult.

> Lord,
>> make me an instrument of your peace:
> where there is hatred,
>> let me sow love;
> where there is doubt,
>> faith;
> where there is sadness,
>> comfort;
> where there is despair,
>> hope;
> where there is death,
>> acceptance and peace.
>
> Grant that I may not:
> so much seek to be consoled,
>> as to console;
> to be understood,
>> as to understand;
> to be loved,
>> as to love.
> For it is in giving
>> that we receive;
> it is in pardoning
>> that we are pardoned;
> and in dying
>> that we are born to eternal life.

Joy begins to mature when the Christian realizes that growth occurs by the grace of the Lord God. Exactly what does growth mean? People usually think of growth in physical terms, yet spiritual growth should be a greater concern to the believer.

Christians often set up scales of spiritual growth to compare one another's spiritual status. Although such evaluation and judgment of other Christians is not scriptural, the Bible does give some standards for self-examination.

Scripture teaches that spiritual growth takes place as the individual continually releases himself to Jesus as Lord. Accepting Christ's lordship means giving *everything* to him. As the Christian releases his physical, mental, emotional, social, financial, and spiritual spheres of life to the Lord, God will mature him according to divine will. Missionary Jim Elliot puts it this way:

> He is no fool who gives up
> That which he cannot keep
> For that which he cannot lose.

A person's growth is sometimes stifled because of difficulties with new challenges that he sees as a frightening threat to his balance or status quo. It is sad that some people act like they would rather live in a miserable condition that is familiar than risk the challenge of a glorious but uncertain future. Especially in troubled times, remember that growth, whether physical or spiritual, is not instantaneously noticeable. Time is required to observe constructive and progressive change. An individual's very process of growing into all that he is meant to be in the Lord God involves its own particular joy.

There are two key characteristics that are essential for growth toward spiritual completeness. The first characteristic is discernment, the ability to see and analyze spiritual matters quickly. Discernment, the God-given ability to have accuracy in discriminating what is not customarily evident to the mind, will sharpen the understanding and make wisdom available to the believer.

The second characteristic, which is essential for spiritual growth, is raw courage. Courage is a difficult matter for most people, simply because they fear risking. Most Christians are not accustomed to taking risks in any areas of their lives. Believers must rely on the Word of God and risk themselves to Jesus as

Savior and Lord. Scripture assures that those who invest in spiritual things will not be disappointed with the spiritual dividend.

SINGLES ALIVE! DECLARATION [5]

Preamble: Whereas the written and spoken word about singles has been and continues to be one of gloom and doom, untruths and misinformation, we the singles of the United States— divorced, separated, widowed, and never-married—in order to bury the myths, establish the truths, uplift our spirits, promote our freedom, become cognizant of our great fortune as singles, do ordain and establish this manifesto for the singles of the United States of America.

ARTICLE I

Attitude toward Self

1. As a single, I shall appreciate myself as a unique person with a special combination of traits and talents that no one else has.

2. I will develop and maintain a healthy self-respect and a high sense of self-worth, knowing that I cannot respect and like others until I first appreciate myself.

3. I will at all times take responsibility for my own actions, knowing that responsibility begins within my own self.

4. I will strive to put all my talents to work so that I can eliminate any residual, socially induced feeling of inferiority, knowing that when I give of myself to others, my self-esteem will rise accordingly.

5. I will have goals, knowing I will feel a sense of elation and heightened self-esteem once the goal is accomplished.

6. I will give myself rewards when I have accomplished a goal or difficult task, knowing the more I practice the spirit of giving to myself, the more I will be able to give to others—and rewards, like charity, begin at home.

7. I will take an entirely new look at loneliness, knowing there is a vast difference between loneliness and being alone, realizing further that loneliness is a part of the human condition and that facing it when it happens will allow me to appreciate the positive side of being alone.

8. I will, in my deepest feelings, know that it's okay to be single and, becoming braver, know that it's even more okay—it can be a great and untapped opportunity for continuous personal growth.

ARTICLE II

Attitude toward Others

1. I will stop searching for the "one-and-only," knowing that as I become more free to be myself, I will be free to care about others, so that relationships will come to me as a natural consequence and I will feel free to accept or reject them.

2. Instead of searching for the "one-and-only," I will realize the tremendous importance of friendships and will develop understanding, worthwhile friends of both the same and opposite sex. I will realize that platonic friendships are not only possible, but a necessary part of a successful single life.

3. I will take inventory of my present friends, bypassing those who are negative and harmful and cultivating those who are helpful and nourishing.

4. I will, when I attend singles' affairs, consider the singles I meet there as potential friends, not as losers, knowing my attitude will color my perception even before I step in the door.

ARTICLE III

Attitude toward Society

1. I will appreciate that all four categories of single people—divorced, separated, widowed, and never-married—suffer discriminations and that we are much more alike than different, no matter what our age or sex.

2. I will appreciate that the so-called battle of the sexes is a social myth, that men and women are much more alike than different in their reactions to fear, rejection, loneliness, sorrow, joy, caring, sharing, and loving, and that, as singles, we have a unique opportunity to foster understanding and empathy between male and female.

3. I will no longer suffer in silence the injustices to me as a single, but will do everything I can to help eradicate them.

4. I will, by choosing to live a free single life, help to raise the status of singlehood. In doing this, I will be strengthening rather than weakening marriage, for when we truly have the option not to marry, marriage will be seen as a free choice rather than a situation demanded by a pairing society.

5. Finally, I will do my part in every way to promote good will between married and single people, because misunderstandings will be diminished only when the members of each group, as unique human beings, realize that being self-aware, autonomous, free, self-fulfilled, and whole have nothing whatsoever to do with either marriage or singleness, but, in the final analysis, come from being ourselves.

CONCLUSION

There is no magic formula in the pages of this book, only the suggestion that every person work hard to reevaluate his own life. What you have learned about yourself in these pages can help you to invest yourself in God's intended work for you. By examining your relationship with God and your attitudes and ideas, you can help God solve your problems rather than causing your own problems.

It is my desire that this work will encourage you to open more to the Lord God so that he can mature you to full personal completeness. Most of what you can learn from what I have said will be transferred to your daily attitudes and actions only if you want it to. If you will try to make these ideas work, you will be rewarded with new insights.

You are probably involved with a group of single adults in your own church. If you and your singles' group will work hard to develop a positive climate of spiritual support, others will naturally desire to affiliate with you. It might be that at first your singles' group will not function exactly as you desire. If so, relax; the important thing is to scripturally care, share, relate, and love the people in your group.

133

Outside your group, neither apologize for your singles nor say "everyone should be like us." Look for those who are interested in relating more deeply. Then you will find more of the support that you need to keep challenging yourself.

An anonymous author wrote a profound poem that concerns evaluating aspects of one's personhood. The truly alive single adult is the one who can look himself straight in the eye in a mirror and know that he is right with God, himself, and others. Your response to this statement will reveal a great deal about your self-awareness and self-acceptance:

When you get what you want in your struggle for life,
And the world makes you king or queen for a day,
Then go to the mirror and look at yourself,
And see what the person there has to say.

For it is not your mother, or father, or spouse,
Who judgment upon you must pass;
The person whose verdict counts most in your life
Is the one staring back from the glass.

He is the person to please, not the rest,
For he is with you clear up to the end.
And you have passed your most dangerous, difficult test,
If the person in the glass is your friend.

You may be like Jack Horner and "chisel" a plum,
And think you are a wonderful person,
But the one in the glass says you are only a bum
If you cannot look him straight in the eye.

You can fool the whole world down the pathway of years
And get pats on the back as you pass,
But your final reward will be heartaches and tears
If you have cheated the person in the glass.

NOTES

1   The concept of the Johari Window of Awareness is thoroughly explained by Luft in *Group Processes: An Introduction to Group Dynamics* (Palo Alto, Calif.: Mayfield Publishing Co., 1970).

2   Personality characteristics and modes of manipulation are discussed by Everett Shostrom in *Man, the Manipulator* (Nashville: Abingdon Press, 1967).

3   This cartoon by Brenda Gire was first published in the newspaper of the First Baptist Church, Chula Vista, Calif., *Our Life Together,* September 7, 1979. Used by permission.

4   The material concerning the four primary stages of a single adult ministry is drawn from a personal interview with R. Kenneth Gunter, September 4, 1982, at Ridgecrest Conference Center, Ridgecrest, North Carolina.

5   The Singles Alive! Declaration is adapted from a book by Marie Edwards and Eleanor Hoover titled *The Challenge of Being Single* (New York: New American Library, 1974), pp. 215–17. Used by permission of J. P. Tarcher.

BIBLIOGRAPHY

The following books should help those who are interested in further reading about living as a Christian single. The bibliography is arranged by the various categories of singleness; resources are also included for personal growth and for those who are working in a singles' ministry in a local church.

Although I recommend all of these books for various reasons, I obviously do not endorse the total contents of every one. The alert reader is urged to discern between those books written from a totally Christian perspective and those not so written.

Never Married Singles

Anders, Sarah Frances. *Women Alone: Confident and Creative.* Nashville: Broadman Press, 1976.

Brock, Raymond T. *Dating and Waiting for Marriage.* Springfield, Mo.: Gospel Publishing House, 1982.

Collins, Gary R. *It's OK to Be Single.* Waco, Tex.: Word, 1976.

Cook, Melva. *Thirty Plus and Single.* Nashville: Convention Press, 1979.

Evening, Margaret. *Who Walk Alone: A Consideration of the Single Life.* Downers Grove, Ill.: Inter-Varsity Press, 1974.

Lawson, Linda. *Life as a Single Adult.* Nashville: Convention Press, 1976.

Mitting, Elizabeth. *The Single Woman: Comments from a Christian Standpoint.* London: Victory Press, 1966.

Satir, Virginia. *Peoplemaking.* Palo Alto, Calif.: Science and Behavior Books, 1972.

Swindoll, Luci. *Wide My World, Narrow My Bed.* Portland, Oreg.: Multnomah, 1982.

Towns, Jim. *One Is Not a Lonely Number.* Dallas: Crescendo Press, 1977.

Witte, Karen. *Great Leaps in a Single Bound.* Minneapolis: Bethany House Publishers, 1982.

Wood, Britton, and Wood, Bobbye. *Marriage Readiness.* Nashville: Broadman Press, 1984.

Divorced Singles

Arnold, William V. *When Your Parents Divorce.* Philadelphia: Westminster Press, 1980.

Besson, Clyde Colvin. *Picking Up the Pieces.* Millford, Mich.: Mott Media, 1982.

Buck, Peggy S. *I'm Divorced—Are You Listening Lord?* Valley Forge, Pa.: Judson Press, 1976.

Crook, Roger H. *An Open Book to the Christian Divorcée.* Nashville: Broadman Press, 1974.

Duty, Guy. *Divorce and Remarriage.* Minneapolis. Bethany Fellowship, 1967.

Ellisen, Stanley A. *Divorce and Remarriage in the Church.* Grand Rapids, Mich.: Zondervan Publishing House, 1977.

Hensley, J. Clark. *Coping with Being Single Again.* Nashville: Broadman Press, 1978.

Hudson, R. Lofton. *'Til Divorce Do Us Part: A Christian Looks at Divorce.* Nashville: Thomas Nelson, 1973.

Lovett, C. S. *The Compassionate Side of Divorce.* Baldwin Park, Calif.: Personal Christianity, 1975.

Martin, John R. *Divorce and Remarriage.* Scottdale, Pa.: Herald Press, 1974.

Peppler, Alice Stewart. *Divorced and Christian.* St. Louis: Concordia Publishing House, 1974.

Small, Dwight H. *The Right to Remarry.* Old Tappan, N.J.: Fleming H. Revell, 1975.

Smoke, Jim. *Growing through Divorce.* Irvine, Calif: Harvest House Publishers, 1976.

Towner, Jason. *Jason Loves Jane. . . . but they got a divorce.* Nashville: Benson Co. 1979.

Wheeler, Michael. *No-Fault Divorce.* Boston: Beacon Press, 1974.

Separated Singles

Chapman, Gary. *Hope for the Separated.* Chicago: Moody Press, 1982.

Gatby, Richard H. *Single Father's Handbook: A Guide for Separated and Divorced Fathers.* Garden City, N.Y.: Anchor Books, 1979.

Weiss, Robert. *Marital Separation.* New York: Basic Books, 1975.

Widowed Singles

Alk, Louis. *How to Be a Successful Widow.* New York: Fleeting Publishing, 1967.

Bogard, David. *Valleys And Vistas: After Losing Life's Partner.* Grand Rapids, Mich.: Baker Book House, 1974.

Brite, Mary. *Triumph over Tears.* Nashville: Thomas Nelson, 1979.

Brown, Velma Darbo. *After Weeping—A Song.* Nashville: Broadman Press, 1980.

Caine, Lynn. *Widow.* New York: Bantam Books, 1975.

Champagne, Marion G. *Facing Life Alone: What Widows and Divorcées Should Know.* Indianapolis: Bobbs-Merrill, 1964.

Jackson, Edgar Newman. *You and Your Grief.* New York: Channel, 1961.

Langer, Marion. *Learning to Live as a Widow.* New York: Mossner, 1957.

Start, Clarissa. *When You're a Widow.* St. Louis: Concordia Publishing House, 1973.

Torrey, Antoinette Walker. *Wisdom for Widows.* New York: E. P. Dutton, 1941.

Towns, Jim. *Faith Stronger Than Death.* Anderson, Ind.: Warner Press, 1975.

Weibe, Katie F. *Alone: A Widow's Search for Joy.* Wheaton, Ill.: Tyndale House, 1976.

Westburg, Granger. *Good Grief.* Philadelphia: Fortress Press, 1962.

Single Parent

Bel Geddes, Joan. *How to Parent Alone: A Guide for Single Parents.* New York: Seabury Press, 1974.

Carter, Velma Thorne, and Leavenworth, J. Lynn. *Putting the Pieces Together.* Valley Forge, Pa.: Judson Press, 1977.

Gardner, Richard A. *The Boys and Girls Book about Divorce.* New York: Bantam Books, 1971.

Gardner, Richard A. *The Parents Book about Divorce.* New York: Doubleday, 1977.

Hensley, J. Clark. *Help for Single Parents and Those Who Love Them.* Jackson, Miss.: Christian Action Commission, 1973.

Hope, Karol, and Young, Nancy, ed. *Momma: The Source Book for Single Mothers.* New York: Polub Books, 1976.

Schlesinger, Benjamin. *The One-Parent Family: Perspectives and Annotated Bibliography.* 3rd ed. Toronto: University of Toronto Press, 1978.

Smith, Charles Edward. *Helps for the Single-Parent Christian Family.* Nashville: Convention Press, 1978. (Teaching tape also available.)

Single Stepparent

Berman, Claire. *Making It as a Stepparent: New Roles/New Rules.* New York: Doubleday, 1980.

Lofas, Jeannette, and Roosevelt, Ruth. *Living in Step.* New York: Stein and Day, 1976.

Ricci, Tsolina. *Mom's House/Dad's House: Making Shared Custody Work.* New York: Macmillan, 1980.

Visher, Emily, and Visher, John. *How to Win as a Stepfamily.* New York: Dembner Books, 1982.

Middle-aged Single

Conway, Jim. *Men in Mid-Life Crisis.* Elgin, Ill.: David C. Cook, 1978.

Conway, Sally. *You and Your Husband's Mid-Life Crisis.* David C. Cook, 1980.

Madden, Myron, and Madden, Mary Ben. *The Time of Your Life.* Nashville: Broadman Press, 1977.

McConnell, Adeline. *Single after Fifty.* New York: McGraw-Hill, 1980.

Rubin, Lillian B. *Women of a Certain Age: The Midlife Search for Self.* New York: Harper and Row, 1979.

Personal Growth for Singles

Allbritton, Cliff. *How to Get Married and Stay That Way*. Nashville: Broadman Press, 1982.

Billheimer, Paul. *Don't Waste Your Sorrows*. Fort Washington, Pa.: Christian Literature Crusade, 1977.

Bonhoeffer, Dietrich. *The Cost of Discipleship*. New York: Macmillan, 1963.

Chambers, Oswald. *My Utmost for His Highest*. New York: Dodd, Mead, 1935.

Chapian, Marie. *Telling Yourself the Truth*. Minneapolis: Bethany House Publishers, 1980.

Clarkson, Margaret. *So You're Single!* Wheaton, Ill.: Harold Shaw, 1978.

Cole, W. Douglas. *Singles: Wants vs. Shoulds*. Nashville: Convention Press, 1980.

Duncan, James E. *The Reason for Joy*. Nashville: Broadman Press, 1978.

Dyer, Wayne W. *Your Erroneous Zones*. New York: Avon Books, 1977.

Eareckson, Joni, and Musser, Joe. *Joni*. Grand Rapids, Mich.: Zondervan Publishing House, 1976.

Eareckson, Joni, and Estes, Steve. *A Step Further*. Grand Rapids, Mich.: Zondervan Publishing House, 1978.

Edman, Raymond. *They Found the Secret*. Grand Rapids, Mich.: Zondervan Publishing House, 1960.

Fix, Janet, and Levitt, Zola. *For Singles Only*. Old Tappan, N.J.: Fleming H. Revell, 1978.

George, Jeannette Clift. *Some Run with Feet of Clay*. Old Tappan, N.J.: Fleming H. Revell, 1979.

Getz, Gene A. *Building Up One Another*. Wheaton, Ill.: Victor Books, 1976.

Getz, Gene A. *The Measure of a Church*. Glendale, Calif.: Regal Books, 1975.

Harbour, Brian. *Famous Singles of the Bible*. Nashville: Broadman Press, 1980.

Hitt, Russell T. *How Christians Grow*. New York: Oxford University Press, 1979.

Hosier, Helen Kooiman. *Forgiveness in Action*. New York: Hawthorn Books, 1974.

Jepson, Sarah. *Devotions for the Single Set*. Carol Stream, Ill.: Creation House, 1972.

LaHaye, Tim. *How to Win Over Depression*. Grand Rapids, Mich.: Zondervan Publishing House, 1974.

Mahoney, James. *Journey into Fullness*. Nashville: Broadman Press, 1974.

Mayeroff, Milton. *On Caring*. New York: Harper and Row, 1971.

McDowell, Josh, and Lewis, Paul. *Givers, Takers, and Other Kinds of Lovers*. Wheaton, Ill.: Tyndale House, 1980.

Narramore, Bruce. *You're Someone Special*. Grand Rapids, Mich.: Zondervan Publishing House, 1978.

Nee, Watchman. *The Normal Christian Life*. Wheaton, Ill.: Tyndale House, 1977.

Powell, John. *Fully Human, Fully Alive*. Niles, Ill.: Argus Communications, 1969.

Robertson, Pat. *The Secret Kingdom*. Nashville: Thomas Nelson, 1982.

Shedd, Charles. *Getting through to the Wonderful You*. Old Tappan, N.J.: Fleming H. Revell, 1976.

Smith, Charles. *Commitment: The Cement of Love*. Nashville: Broadman Press, 1982.

Stevens, Velma Darbo. *A Fresh Look at Loneliness*. Nashville: Broadman Press, 1981.

Strebeck, Mary. *Single . . . But Not Alone*. Brentwood, Tenn.: J M Publications, 1982.

Swindoll, Charles. *Improving Your Serve*. Waco, Tex.: Word, 1981.

Talley, Jim. *Too Close Too Soon*. Nashville: Thomas Nelson, 1982.

Towns, Jim. *Life: Joy in Being*. Nashville: Convention Press, 1981.

Towns, Jim. *Solo Flight*. Wheaton, Ill.: Tyndale House, 1980.

Yohn, Rick. *Discover Your Spiritual Gift and Use It*. Wheaton, Ill.: Tyndale House, 1982.

Single Leadership

Craig, Floyd A. *How to Communicate with Single Adults*. Nashville: Broadman Press, 1978.

Lawson, Linda, ed. *Working with Single Adults in Sunday School: Resource Kit*. Nashville: Convention Press, 1978.

Potts, Nancy D. *Counseling with Single Adults*. Nashville: Broadman Press, 1978.

Smith, Ann Alexander. *How to Start a Single Adult Ministry*. Nashville: Baptist Sunday School Board (Materials Services Department, 127 Ninth Avenue North, 37234).

Smith, Ann Alexander. *Divorce Adjustment Workshop: A Guide for Leaders*. Nashville: Baptist Sunday School Board.

Towns, Jim, and Strebeck, Mary. *Single . . . But Not Alone: Leadership Study Guide.* Brentwood, Tenn.: J M Publications, 1983.

Wood, Britton. *Single Adults Want to Be in the Church, Too.* Nashville: Broadman Press, 1977.

March, 1986

Interesting book! Jim Towns
Writes as a christian, who
Went through a lot of the self
doubt and misunderstandings
that I went through as I chose
to give up on my marriage.
In my memory the good things
get cloudy when you've
experienced the hurt and the
distance from your spouse.
It's important as Jim Towns
writes not to harbor those
hurt feelings but to pick up
and go on with your life.
Getting a divorce made me
closer to God as so many
days while I was married I
didn't feel close to God. But
now my God, my kids and
my family are my support
Group and all I need.